C & H
✓ 3 95

W9-BQL-705

66 - 15750 (10 - 20 - 66)

THE YOUNG NEGRO IN AMERICA: 1960–1980

The Young Negro

in America:
1960-1980

by Samuel D. Proctor

ASSOCIATION PRESS | **NEW YORK**

WINGATE COLLEGE LIBRARY
WINGATE, N. C.

To my devoted wife

THE YOUNG NEGRO IN AMERICA: 1960–1980

Copyright © 1966 by
National Board of Young Men's Christian Associations

Association Press, 291 Broadway, New York, N.Y. 10007

All rights reserved, including the right of reproduction in whole or in part in any form, under the International, Pan-American, and Universal Copyright Conventions.

Publisher's stock number: 1611

Library of Congress catalog card number: 66–15750

Printed in the United States of America

Preface

In early February, 1960, on a bright Saturday made quiet by a steady snowfall, sixteen presidents of Negro colleges sat chatting leisurely over post-lunch coffee, crumpled linen napkins, and empty steak plates in a well-appointed room on the rural campus of Maryland State College. That campus is two miles east of Highway 13 at Princess Anne. The men were the heads of institutions comprising the membership of the half-century-old CIAA, Central (formerly Colored) Intercollegiate Athletic Association. At this meeting the presidents had gone into their annual huddle to make athletic policy as a kind of caucus before the formal meeting of the Association in March where coaches—not presidents—would call the plays.

Such a background is needed to focus on the semiclandestine nature of this meeting of the sixteen Negro Ph.Ds.

While they talked about football, buses, changing linens for visiting teams, halfbacks, and alumni resolutions after losing seasons, withdrawn securely from their various publics by the isolation of that tidy campus and protected further from the casual intruder by the sheets of clean white snow, a waiter pushed a door wide open and barked a telephone call for one of the North Carolina presidents. College presidents know how crisis-prone a campus is, and they leap with alarm to take an out-of-town call from the halls of ivy back home.

When this president returned to the room with a blank stare on his face, his own response was quickly multiplied when he announced to his colleagues that his students had been jailed by the scores in a sit-in demonstration.

The tempo and the subject matter of the meeting was changed with lightening abruptness. The genial hilarity turned to near grief.

32692

Without anyone saying what he was doing, everyone began to fold his papers stealthily, sneaking a glance at his watch to gauge the driving time home, for it was an open secret that when this movement began it would spread with rapid contagion to every other Negro campus.

The trivia of football discussions evaporated, and the room became intellectually sterilized with ideas of surgical seriousness. The issue no longer was how many guards, tackles, coaches, and trainers could be housed by a host team, but how much momentum had this brazen movement gathered and how much disruption would it create in the college towns; not how much money should be spent for fleet-footed pass-hawking ends, but how much of the leadership of the status Negro had already been lost to this new breed that had taken the Negro struggle from the Sunday afternoon forum to the streets and the jails. The question was not how these Negro colleges could maintain their academic integrity with growing athletic establishments, but how long the Negro world—colleges, barber shops, lodges, cemeteries, and churches—would remain intact after this bold drive toward full integration into the total fabric of American life had just made its first major thrust.

As these men solemnly closed their meeting, leaving their agenda half finished, to separate for the journey home, it was like the reluctance of friends turning away from the winter burial of a buddy to begin the slow melting process of bereavement.

Indeed it was a funeral, the death of an old, old familiar pattern of life in America. It had lost its vitality and had come to the hardening of its arteries. Its power to endure had become insufficient, and its time had run out. It was common knowledge that it would die sooner or later, but no one would dare lift a hand to kill it. It died slowly, and if there was any question as to the exact date of its demise, there was no doubt that the funeral of the "discussion method of status changing for the Negro" was held on that snowy Saturday in February when the Negro college presidents were in their annual football meeting.

This football conference had a definite place in the old order of things. Negro life has always embraced a parallel to every phase of the culture in the dominant American tradition—fraternities, formal dances, weekend poker parties, church raffles, conspicuous consumption, plaques for mediocre achievements, or whatever you may name. This meeting of the presidents of Negro colleges to discuss a revision in athletic policies was conducted within the broad frame of reference of Negro life in 1960. Negro institutions had grown and developed for a hundred years; and, although discussion of integration had accelerated, nowhere was there any considerable support among educated, status-bound, professional Negroes for an overt showdown with segregation at the front door of restaurants or at the gates of country clubs. They had applauded the victories of their cause in the courts and in the Congress, but they had tabled indefinitely the notion that southern whites would surrender without force and violence, and they were therefore continuing with business as usual, football included.

Picketing, mass protests, and demonstrations had been associated in the minds of status Negroes with odd types—the mavericks, the leftists, the political opportunists, and the neurotic radicals. Just how they expected change to come was never clear, even though the groundwork was being laid constantly. This is the question the college students had asked themselves and on that Saturday in February, 1960, they resolved that the spiral of logic had spun to a dead halt. The next step was to go on and stage impromptu, unrehearsed integration. And the following step was to let the courts, the communities, and the college presidents catch up with their presumptuousness.

It is risky to ascribe so much significance to a single step in a major social change. There were other personalities who were effective in their own day, and this emphasis upon the young Negro may tend to obscure their contribution. Nevertheless, the dramatic shift in Negro strategy—more iconoclastic by far than a boycott—came with the jailing of college students in 1960. The thesis can be defended that the shift resulted in the awakening of the churches on this issue, the 1963 March on Washington, the 1964 Civil Rights Bill, the 1964 Equal Opportunity Act, and the 1965 Voting Rights Act.

Any literate Negro feels almost reverent toward the brave and creative early pioneers of the freedom movement, from Nat Turner and Richmond's Gabriel all the way to Charles Houston and Walter White. This has been a long train of courageous and sensitive souls who felt the pain and the anguish of racism gnawing at their viscerals and disturbing their minds since the first slave ship landed its cargo on these shores. We cannot forget those who labored in the quarry when the rock was hard. This generation of young Negroes needs to be reminded that it stands on the shoulders of others and that the vistas that have beckoned to them have been made visible to their youthful eyes only because to their own height there is added the height of tall men and women who have gone before.

The story of the historical antecedents to February, 1960, makes—and has made—many other books. Our purpose here is to look at the young Negro who took that giant step in 1960, to assess his strength and his purposes, and to conjecture where he will be by, let us say, 1980.

In a sense this book gets written in every declaration at a Harlem bar about what the Negro is ready to do to attain his full freedom. Every suburban conversation that raises the issue of how far Negroes really want to go is part of the subject of this book. Every sermon that calls for commitment to full emancipation contributes to this topic. Every foundation grant that seeks to raise the level of performance of Negro students is a part of the story.

This book is a projection—a short-range prognostication. How far will the young Negro seek to go by 1980? What effort will it require on his part? How prepared is he to pay the price? What will it require of business, government, religion, education, and other social institutions? Will the responses be adequate?

What does one expect to accomplish with this type of projection? Hopefully, the young Negro and his allies will find here an appraisal of what this drive will demand if it maintains its splendid pace. The book makes an estimate of the tremendous historical yardage that can be gained if this pace is kept up to 1980, when those who were sophomores in 1960 will be parents of sophomores, managers of the nations's business, and leaders in the body politic. Hopefully, those who are now managers and leaders may share in this appraisal and help to write a chapter in American history more glorious than we have seen before, a chapter that will truly reflect the fulfillment of the promises in the Declaration of Independence.

The author acknowledges his debt to Loretta Jenkins for typing the manuscript and to Gregory F. Simms, Georgianna Shine McGuire, Ralph D. Matthews, Jr., and Sherry Turner for criticizing the first draft. Responsibility for the views that follow, however, rests upon the author.

Contents

1

The Emergence of the Young Negro

SINCE 1960 we have witnessed a rather steady, slow, but unbroken pace in changing the status of the American Negro. From one headline to another, from city to city, from month to month, we have found the old image of "the colored" being etched over by new forms and new symbols. What was taken for granted as a permanent, enduring social arrangement, with Negroes notched securely in a groove of inferiority, turned out actually to be a long pause between emancipations.

The Bid for a New Emancipation

Several tributaries, flowing from springs revived by currents of post-World War II history, all seemed to rush toward the confluence of the young Negro's vigorous bid for a new emancipation in 1960. Hardly anyone believed that placid segregation and rigid job discrimination could go on much longer after the hopeful promise that the Negro found in the 1954 school decision. But who would make the first move? Who would risk his security by sounding an alarm that would turn America around, full circle, in matters of race?

With white liberals thinly scattered, with the Negro who had arrived frantically striving to hold his gains, with government, business, and industry reflecting the status quo, what was needed was a fresh, new ingredient. It would have to be solvent and powerful enough to be the catalyst that would activate dormant American idealism, the aspirations of the Negroes, and the virility that this strong nation always shows best under a challenge.

The spring semester of 1960 saw every one of the sixty-odd Negro colleges of the South beset with the confusion and disorder that accompanied the participation of students in civil rights demonstrations. From February through June no one knew what to expect, because the students had taken over and the weight of morality was on their side. The administrators were standing on tiptoe, watching for the next move. All the arguments that deans, trustees, and presidents used to persuade students to return to their classrooms, laboratories, and term papers were used by students against these adult advisers to indict them as gradualists, at best, and as "handkerchief heads," at worst.

When school opened in September, a president who thought himself to be still in contact with student leadership called one of the leaders of the demonstrations into his office for a quiet, informal chat. It was not unusual for a student leader to be asked to drop by for such a talk. Indeed, this president enjoyed a reputation for being the kind of contemporary spirit who could talk with the young. He reminded this student leader that he had five incomplete grades for the five courses that he had taken in the spring semester. He cautioned him to focus attention on his school work in the fall semester and let others pick up the leadership in the "movement."

"What good is a degree," the student replied, "if I don't have my freedom?"

The remark shocked the president into an awareness of the twenty years that separated him from this student in spite of the fact that both of them were wearing the same style of sport coat, tight trousers, and hand-sewn moccasins. Politically, socially, and psychologically they were strangers; and nothing like small talk about football, music, or summer travel could bridge the chasm that separated them.

The president could not accept this alienation. It was not antipathy toward him as a person but impatience and contempt for his entire generation. The president belonged to a responsible but nevertheless outmoded school of thought. He had been a student of the civil rights movement and had seen the NAACP win forty or more successive cases before the Supreme Court, inching the Negro closer and closer toward full civil liberty. He made fifty-odd speeches to interracial groups every year and had bowed to the applause of the most congenial whites anyone would want to meet. He had been bold in question-and-answer periods, exclaiming that the time had come for full emancipation without further delay. His faculty was free to make speeches anywhere on any topic without fear of reprisal. He had defended the students' right to demonstrate as long as they were orderly and, more than that, he had arranged a system for providing bond when students were arrested en masse.

In terms of full emancipation, he believed that the best strategy for the individual Negro was to gain as much education, approval, and mannerliness as he could and to be prepared for the day when the managers of government, business, and industry would give the nod. He could not conceive of the Negro people pricking the conscience of white America with sit-ins and compelling government agencies, churches, political parties, corporations, and foundations to change their philosophies and to make a sincere effort to renovate long-standing patterns in race relations. Though this president felt the moral obligation to support the students in their demonstrations, he was not convinced that such efforts would do anything more than create headlines, add another year of college for those who participated, keep the chief of police awake for several nights, cause the mayor to lose his vacation, give students some rehearsal in elocution, provide a substitute for "panty raids" and dormitory water fights, suggest new dissertation topics for psychology Ph.D. candidates, and consolidate the threatening growth of rabid segregationists.

These students had an excellent reading on their adult contemporaries. In fact, they knew so well what the adult sentiment was that they would not permit themselves to be dragged into extensive conversation. They seemed to know that the support they had received was perfunctory and heartless. They seemed to know also that in order for their point of view to be understood one would have to be young, without a substantial annual salary to protect, without a mortgage to pay, without a wife and children to

WINGATE COLLEGE LIBRARY
WINGATE, N. C.

support, and without much concern for other penalties for iconoclastic activity. Since their adult contemporaries were weighted
down with all these inhibiting conditions, there was really not
much point in talking with them at all. So they held their meetings
under clandestine arrangements, plotted strategies, and executed
them in the most disciplined manner.

The Influence of Earlier Demonstrations

The demonstrations of the Negro college students which began
in 1960 were unique in many ways, but this phenomenon was by
no means the first bold effort made to accomplish social and political goals in the Negro's behalf. Perhaps the most successful of
such demonstrations was the one that never came off. During
World War II, A. Philip Randolph, president of the Brotherhood
of Sleeping Car Porters, threatened to mobilize a hundred thousand Negroes and march to Washington to protest unfair employment practices. In response to this proposal, President Franklin D.
Roosevelt issued Executive Order 8802 which created a Federal
Fair Employment Practices Committee to correct discriminatory
practices in defense production.

There can be little doubt that the Montgomery Bus Boycott led
by Martin Luther King inspired the young Negro to accelerate the
pace in the civil rights drive. Nevertheless, there are other factors
to be considered, for Martin Luther King's demonstrations in
Montgomery were not the first in recent times. An earlier generation saw how Mary Church Terrell led demonstrations in the
District of Columbia to integrate restaurants. Adam Clayton
Powell led protest demonstrations against job discrimination in
Harlem. A few months before King's demonstrations against bus
segregation, Reverend Theodore J. Jemison had led similar demonstrations in Baton Rouge, Louisiana.

Of course, the whole idea of dramatizing a social wrong by mass
demonstrations is a story in itself. More than 150 years ago hundreds of thousands of persons protested the British slave trade by
refusing to use sugar in their tea. This movement was directed
against the sugar plantations in the West Indies where slavery was
deeply entrenched.

Therefore, in addition to the impetus of Martin Luther King's leadership, one must consider the entire mood of the Negro following the 1954 school decision. There was a great deal of activity within the Negro communities. Oratory ran high, and indignation over continued segregation reached the boiling point. A new boldness was seen on every hand, and something had to give. The fact that the politicians and the white power structure remained unaware of this only signified the hopeless social distance that separated the Negroes and the whites in large urban centers where the Negro population is better than one-third.

In city after city, respected and trusted Negro leadership was called downtown to sit with business leaders around heavy oak tables in paneled offices with the velvet touch. They were called even to the synagogues where on supposedly neutral ground some speedy rapprochement could be achieved. They heard men experienced in "dealing with the colored" exclaim that these new developments would merely destroy "lines of communication." They found it hard to accept that it was the very purpose of Negroes after 1954 to see those old lines of communication destroyed and replaced by new and clearer lines through which a new message could be gotten across without static or distortion.

Harry Golden*[1] reports a meeting called by Governor Hugh White of Mississippi to ask Negro leaders to give their support to a voluntary segregation plan. In return, the Governor promised to upgrade the Negro schools and make them equal to those for whites. Only one Negro out of the ninety agreed. The others went off and prepared a statement declaring that they were unsympathetic with any move to circumvent the decision of the Supreme Court. When the Governor received the statement he was stunned.

The young Negro took things into his own hands because discussion, meetings, and oratory had reached their maximal usefulness. The case was clear-cut. The adult Negroes had talked themselves into doing something, but what needed to be done apparently was not the work of men with families, debts, and insecurity. The adult Negro was helplessly dependent upon the approbation of the white power structure. Most families could not afford to miss a single paycheck and, though no one wished to verbalize this inexorable condition, it was an eloquent, still, small voice.

---

* All numbered notes are found at the rear of the book.

The Adult Negro Community in 1960

More should be said regarding this adult Negro community from which the young Negro bolted. It is an unfortunate oversimplification to label the southern Negro adult as "Uncle Tom," who has managed to keep a good job, pay for real estate, educate his children, and maintain a respectable reputation in town. Every town in the South has a Negro community which is held together and given what little self-respect it has by the leadership of this stable element. Beyond the circle of the high school principals, the dentists, the preachers, the physicians, and the undertakers, there is a thin circle of relatively well-employed persons, railroad employees, federal and municipal employees, small businessmen, and even those who have made a career of personal services to very wealthy whites.

To find these people one must visit the larger churches on a Sunday morning and observe those who are in charge. Every September the children of these families are scattered among the sixty Negro college campuses of the South. These people have their own clubs, lodges, social activities, and, increasingly, their own financial institutions. More important, however, is the fact that they have sanctions among themselves, an unwritten code of moral and social behavior. This code is a blending of Christian ethics, middle-class prudence and sobriety, and a discreet response to white power. Many of these people have spent their entire lifetime without giving a single serious thought to the question of revolting against patterns of segregation. They have talked about it among themselves and discussed it supinely. Leaders in church and civil life spoke to them on the theme constantly, but they habitually returned to business as usual because no practical alternative to successful accommodation within the Negro community seemed viable.

Patterns of success were clearly outlined. Families involved in crime and civil suits for bad debts were held in disrepute. Drinking excessively and sexual licentiousness were frowned upon even though it was commonly known that many persons who could afford the privacy and the necessary anonymity indulged in both. Sending children to college was a must, and owning one's home was an indispensable requirement for self-respect. Every family in this stratum had to have its name in the deed book in City Hall.

There were the families who visited their cousins in northern communities in the summer but who had no interest in living in a cluttered place like Harlem or South Philadelphia. It was quite common to hear them speak critically of their relatives who were "piled up" in apartments in the North. Yet one could not say that these people were satisfied. Beneath the surface of accommodation there were the rumblings of discontent over their second-class status. The young Negro could feel this inertia without indicting his parents. He had bitter animosity toward those who *advocated* a "go slow" policy, but there was no antipathy against those who merely *practiced* a "go slow" policy.

The young Negro saw nothing happening among his adult leaders beyond meetings and testimonials to racial chauvinism. He saw nothing happening on the part of the federal government, big business, the major foundations, and the churches. He knew that the Negro had made great strides under Franklin D. Roosevelt, but he wondered what would happen with another eight years like the Eisenhower Administration. President Eisenhower was held in respect, but it was generally conceded that his heart was not with the Negroes and their aspirations toward immediate and full citizenship. Negroes admired the liberal leadership of Adlai Stevenson and they recognized that his candidacy in 1952 and in 1956 had polarized the persons responsive to vigorous Negro advancement on the one hand and those who were indifferent or hostile toward the Negroes on the other. The fact that President Eisenhower was the candidate of those who were largely resistant to the changes sought by the Negroes left them feeling cool toward him as President.

Again and again, incidents reported in the press signified that President Eisenhower was lukewarm toward the Negro. His declarations that brotherhood could not be legislated irritated the Negroes. They had already seen what integration in the Armed Forces had produced and what the FEPC during the war had accomplished. They learned also that when Governor Burns invited President Eisenhower to speak in Columbia, South Carolina, this World War II national hero leaped to attention when the band played Dixie. They knew that when President Eisenhower spoke to a conference of Negro leaders in Washington he advocated a policy of deference to segregationists right to their faces. They knew also that the Vice-President's Commission on Contracts had all but lain dead in the face of flagrant racial discrimination in industries doing business with the federal government. In general, the young Negro expected very little from Washington.

The young Negro of 1960 did not strike out to organize more youth chapters of the NAACP or the Urban League, for here again he believed the adults in charge of these groups to be inextricably bound to the will of the white majority. He feared that entanglement with these organizations would inevitably result in a polite form of delay and the prolongation of the system he deplored.

The Church as the Young Negro Saw It

Not only had they become immune to theological clichés and to the enigmatic, medieval salvation prescriptions preached in the churches, but they sensed something else. The Negro church was a "soul" institution, a haven for those who wanted a refuge from the conflicts and the acrobatics of getting along in the cruel world. Negroes who do hard menial labor all week are tired by Sunday, in body and in spirit, and their churches are refreshment stations, not forums for debating and resolving social issues. The young Negro was familiar with the atmosphere of Mount Zion on Sunday morning, and this was not what he had in mind at all. By its very nature it was a comfortable institution and could not invert its form and structure to become an institution for social change. It eased the pain while some other agent would have to handle the pathology and the therapy. This analgesic role of the church seemed to be conceded by the young Negro without contest. As Kenneth B. Clark, the renowned Negro psychologist, says, "If one demands that the Negro give up the Negro Church before total integration is achieved, on the grounds of consistency with the goals of the civil rights movement, the demand will be rejected, for the Negro has managed to salvage some personal self-esteem from his church . . . his last and only sanctuary."[2]

Though the young Negro did not look to the church, the freest institution that Negroes had, many who were involved in the leadership of the protest movements were loyal church members, active in youth organizations and products of the Sunday school. They had successfully compartmentalized religion in their minds. They had outgrown the biblical literalism of their Sunday school teachers and the salvation formulas that their pastors and parents espoused, but they had not outgrown the church. It was in "churchliness" that they found the ideas and rituals that supported human goodness, the warm fellowship of the best people in town, and the awareness that the world and history were both sustained by an Undefined Power for good. The details they found confusing and incongruous with their midtwentieth century intellectual orientation.

Their immunity to the anesthetic influences of rural, Protestant otherworldliness may be attributed also to the fact that this generation has missed that religious grooming experienced by their teachers, who were only one generation removed from the pious teaching missionaries who came South during the Reconstruction to guide Negro education. The young Negro could not identify any major civil rights leadership in the churches other than Martin Luther King with a program to match his level of determination.

The Fearless Determination of the Young Negro

As we assess the significance of the timing, the strategy, and the atmosphere of the action of the young Negro, we must remember that in early 1960 there were some racial themes being played to which the young Negro wrote the counterpoint. For one thing, many mature and respected adults were cautioning that King-type demonstrations would lead to violence on the part of white hoodlums and the young Negro would be left unprotected and victimized. The young Negroes replied that they were ready to die for their freedom.

As adult Negroes listened to their white friends decry the worsening in race relations, they counseled their children that tensions were mounting and that a prior emphasis should be placed upon reducing these tensions. The young Negro replied that the only way to reduce tensions would be to acquiesce to ongoing white supremacy. They considered the tensions wholesome and creative, a necessary concomitant to the freedom drive.

Other spiritually minded leaders cautioned that the hearts of men needed to be changed first and the young Negro should seek to win the love, the respect, and the admiration of his white neighbors before he forced himself upon them. The young Negro replied that the moral failure on the part of the white majority left them in no position to judge the conduct, motives, or the manners of Negroes.

Others preached that the South needed a "breather" after the Supreme Court decision. The young Negro replied that the whites had used the one hundred years since the Civil War to devise every means possible to create a disadvantaged situation for the Negroes. More time would simply mean the extension of the entire process of discriminatory treatment. It was argued that customs could not be changed overnight. It was argued further that the whites had been reared innocently in a system of a dual society and that this had been ground into their nervous system. It could not be eliminated immediately. The young Negro replied that the longer the system lasted the more indelible the customs would become, and the sooner the system began to undergo change the earlier the whites could begin to get accustomed to the new arrangement.

A rather sophisticated argument was that before further activity there should be the restoration of communication. This was based on the assumption that if whites really knew what Negroes were feeling and thinking they would react with novel ideas for social reorganization and avoid the chaos that was bound to come. Whites and Negroes who once met together could no longer find each other, it was argued. The young Negro replied that the nature of Negro-white communication had been one of condescension and deception. It was not worth restoring, and a new level of communication would follow after the securing of certain basic rights. When they were told that the whites were not emotionally prepared for so radical a change, they replied that neither were Negroes emotionally prepared to continue the way things were. There was lack of preparation on both sides and it was better, therefore, to go with the side of justice, not of emotions.

When the young Negro took over the leadership in the civil rights struggle, he did so without regard for the security of his parents. He was in a revolutionary mood and he recognized that major social surgery would require some loss of blood. He was unconvinced that his actions would bog down in failure, and he was willing to mortgage his future and the security of his parents for the sake of change and a better way of life eventually.

The level of seriousness with which they went about their business won the respect of their most severe critics. They proceeded with their sit-ins, singing freedom songs in jail, and discussing social history with the wardens and the police chiefs.

The young Negro gained such pre-eminence as the new voice and the new force that he developed a suspicion for his next rival, Martin Luther King. Among the college-bred there were no consistent stand-outs, no long-term headliners. King stayed in the press and stole their thunder constantly. Yet this did not cause disaffection for King's position of nonviolence. One cannot overemphasize the providential sequence that brought King to the front in the late fifties as a kind of overture before the debut of the young Negro in 1960. King not only embraced the concept of nonviolence for himself, but propagandized this moral ideal as a weapon of indisputable consequence. In a telegram to Mrs. Daisy Bates during the Little Rock school integration crisis, King advised: "Urge the people of Little Rock to adhere vigorously to a way of nonviolence at this time. I know this is difficult advice. . . . But nonviolence is the only way to a lasting solution of the problem. . . ."[3]

Because of the attitude of nonviolence shown by college demonstrators, much of the reaction that the various communities had every reason to expect never developed. In Greensboro, North Carolina, the chief of police gave highest praises to his collegebred inmates. He remarked over and over again, in private and in public, that he was compelled to respect these young people and the manner in which they embraced their cause. This was indeed something new for college students, for their college town had become accustomed to panty raids, wild parties after football games, and the tears of parents while bailing out their young after arrests for drunkenness or vandalism. In contrast, these Negro students had dedicated themselves to the destruction of an old social order that threatened to confer upon them a lifetime of denial and personal indignity.

The Tempo of the 1960 Negro Student

One begins to understand the tempo of the 1960 Negro student when it is recalled that the Negro college students of 1960 were the children of the World War II veterans. Many were the orphans of men who died on the beach at Normandy, in the North African campaign, and in North Burma. The conversations that these youngsters had heard at the breakfast table and while lying on the living-room rug during the long winter evenings caused them to question seriously the indefinite continuation of racial segregation. They found nothing in logic or in human experience to warrant spending their lives on the explicit assumption that there was something inherently inferior about a person who happened to be born a Negro. They were not convinced of any innate unworthiness; nor were they convinced of any innate superiority on the part of white neighbors. They never considered any alternatives to a program of reconstructing the mores of America in relation to the issue of race.

Their contest was not waged against the structure of the white world. When the young Negroes asked to worship in southern churches, to ride in any seat on the buses, to eat at the counters in department stores, and to swim in public pools, they were not seeking to destroy anything but to affirm the worthwhileness of the white man's culture. They were quite happy with capitalism, Christianity, and the Constitution. They could never have been accused of sedition or treason. In fact, they validated the white world's success symbols and its philosophy of life. They just wanted "in."

Some apostles of Negritude had sought to question this tacit approval of the white man's universe, but this argument had not impressed the young Negro. Even an angry young man like James Baldwin, in his report[4] on the Conference of Negro-African Writers and Artists held at the Sorbonne in 1956, found it difficult to understand a speech by Alioune Diop, editor of *Présence Africaine*. Diop deplored the attitude of some Congolese who wanted total assimilation with white culture. Baldwin argued that he could not see the issue so clearly separated—total assimilation versus total rejection of Western culture. Today, ten years later, there seems to be much more black chauvinism abroad than there was in 1956 or 1960, but the posture of the young Negro in the leadership in 1960 was one of moving toward—rather than in an alternate direction— the same escalator that climbed up the stages of success that the whites had invented.

Admittedly, there is something about the young which is irrational, a capacity for impulsive activity which throws caution to the wind. Youth requires its own self-identification, its own dances, music, jargon, style of dress, and a characteristic revolt against adult sanctions. But the young Negro in his drive for civil rights defied these classical characterizations of the young. His cause was deeply rooted in logic, in history; and it was a responsible activity. It did not involve breaking the windows of the homes of the college presidents, turning over automobiles, and storming public buildings. It was an organized effort, consummated in endless meetings and debates. It was disciplined, calculated, and deliberate. It was executed with calmness and self-assurance. It disarmed all its adversaries.

Although it can be said that the American Negro has had only passing interest in Africa, it is true that the successful accomplishment of independence on the part of African nations caused the American Negro to feel ashamed of his continuing resignation to segregation. The young Negroes who made the bold moves toward full emancipation knew the names of the African leaders and were eager to learn more about them. African students on their campuses were largely the products and the beneficiaries of the mission boards and, therefore, really did not represent the militancy that the American Negro admired among Africans. He was interested in the political leadership of the young nations and the psychological stance that one had to assume in order to brace himself to fight with selfless abondonment until a complete victory was achieved. He saw this among the political leaders of Africa, and this caused him for the first time to become emotional about his African heritage. The American Negro identifies only superficially with Africa, but it is inescapable that the drama of the independence of African nations stirred the hearts of the young Negroes and encouraged them in their movements.

So much has happened within recent years in the whole field of race relations that it is difficult to bring oneself again to that precipice on which the Negro people stood when the young Negro became conspicuous as a new factor to be dealt with. The young Negro was perceptive enough to see that the whole structure of segregation was morally corrosive and vulnerable. He was confident that the only support that the old order could count on was the cowardice of frightened Negroes and the violence of racist whites. The legal substructure had been undermined by the 1954 Supreme Court decision and only the phoniest arguments could be given in support of a perpetual dual society. The anthropology behind it was spurious, and the climate of world opinion regarding the dark-skinned people of the world made it anachronistic. The literature of the times produced growing evidence that the bad statistics on the Negro community were the outgrowth of deprivation, poverty, and unequal educational opportunity.

There remained only one course to be followed, and that was a bold break with the past, a direct confrontation with the system, regardless of the cost.

The violence which erupted in the summers of 1964 and 1965, following the impressive March on Washington in 1963 and back-to-back with the passing of the 1964 Civil Rights Bill, was conceived in the same womb of social unrest, weariness with separateness, impatience with being poor and with the boredom of the gray slums, but fertilized by a different sperm. They had a common *maternity* but a different *paternity*. The first Negro demonstrators in Greensboro, Richmond, Nashville, and Atlanta could not be called looters, hoodlums, or pathological arsonists and snipers. They vetoed the impulse to play havoc with the quiet orderliness of southern towns lined with graceful magnolia trees. They constrained themselves magnificently.

They sensed that it would be greatly to their advantage to hold on to the lead on the moral scoreboard. They knew of the white gangster world, white slavery controlled by Caucasians, the dope rings and gambling cartels that were kept intact by unsolved murders and blackmail. They had the gruesome history of the sadistic lynchings well remembered, the orgiastic beatings that often culminated in the emasculation of Negro men. They knew the history of some of the labor unions and the sorry tale of machine gun rule in the worse ones. They knew how violence had been used in America by whites to embarrass the rule of law in almost every aspect of the society, from prize fighting to public elections, from labor bargaining to milk prices. But they wanted the psychological advantage of a clean fight and instinctively they chose the course of passive resistance that generated unassailable moral support.

It is an unfortunate, but an understandable, fact of history that the young Negroes from the urban slums could not appreciate the importance of this moral edge and played into the hands of their enemies by resorting to violence. There simply had not been enough capable leadership to spread around, and men like Dr. King could stay in one town only so long. Other leadership was there in every town, but it had no such magic as King's name had after dozens of arrests, a Harlem waltz with death, three times or more on *Time*'s cover, in the press everyday for seven moving years, a Nobel prize, a great mind, a way with people, and a Boston Ph.D. in Hegelianism. Thus, local leadership failed in trying to match the King image; and the vacuum was too often filled with hotheaded, ambitious, superfluous noisemakers who knew the depths of social wrong but who knew only the clumsiest ways out. Hence the riots.

Yet, even the hotheaded, misguided noisemakers could not incite a riot if the people had no appetite for rioting. This is the subtle but all-important difference between the offspring of middle-class Negroes who led the student revolt on southern Negro college campuses and the young descendants of the rural, uneducated migrants who did not have the protective veneer of college enrollment to shield them from the abrasions of Yankee racism.

These young urban Negroes not only nurture their deep resentment of whites but they have had experience in violence, in gang wars, and in juvenile crime. Their exclusion from the center of society has given them license to indulge in a kind of separate world with a separate law enforced by personal fear and the delicate balance of power between gangs armed with chains, automobile radio aerials, and an assortment of knives and zip guns. This potential has been known for years, and the conditions that permitted it have been left unchanged.

But somehow the education of policemen and police chiefs has been woefully inadequate in race relations. A Negro police officer in a town of 250,000 told friends in an intimate social gathering how a young, white patrolman wanted some shoes found at a crime scene sent to the FBI to see if the odor on them was colored or white. This was a dead give-away. He was going to use that shiny badge and that big gun, perhaps unwittingly, to enforce two brands of law, one for those who "smelled colored" and one for those who "smelled white." The millions of Negroes who are as much as one-eighth to one-half of Caucasian descent must have had a "blended odor." It takes police action by men like that either to set off the tinder box of resentment or to create the atmosphere in which another enlightened officer becomes the spark while making a routine investigation or arrest.

Once the young Negroes started they were ruthless in dismissing their critics. They regarded Negro apostles of caution as children screaming and yelling in the dark when a fuse blows out. They laughed at them. They looked upon the newspaper editors who abused them relentlessly as stooges of their bosses who had no alternative but to violate conscience and intelligence to keep a desk. They looked upon other young Negroes who obeyed their parents and stayed out of the movement as stupid and incapable of self-direction. The passivity of their professors and other status-bound Negroes was understood on economic grounds. Southern politicians who vilified them were categorized as those who would stone the prophets all over again and lead Jesus of Nazareth to Golgotha any Friday of the year. They believed that upper-class whites cared no more for them than they cared for poor whites, and their indifference toward their cause was interpreted as the natural fruit of the matrix of original sin, by which no one except the spiritual elite gives up a known advantage for a known disadvantage.

They knew of the brave stand of several whites who came from the American Friends Service Committee, the Southern Regional Council, and a few from labor, the university communities, and the churches. But there was so much inertia on the part of educated, church-going whites that the few who stood out seemed hopelessly outnumbered. There was nothing like enough activity to allay the fears that segregation was going to remain deeply entrenched until a major confrontation dragged it out for exposure and destruction.

Many of these college students had come from middle-class Negro enclaves in the North, and they pitied their northern counterparts who had been duped into believing that their condition was different from those of the South. They were never more correct, for it was the agitation of the young Negro in the South, who sounded the alarm for Negro communities throughout the nation, and America will never be the same again.

2

Responses to the Freedom Thrust

REACTIONS to the aggressive moves of the young Negroes
have been so multifaceted that a chronological sequence is impossible. There has been a surge of confidence in the hearts of Negro
people mixed with an undertow of cynicism. Raised expectations
have been buffeted by the stirrings of white resentment and the
hate tide coming to the surface. Middle-class Negroes, white
liberals, and church leaders have been compelled to take clearer
stands; and mere academic interest in change has become less and
less tenable. Government, business, philanthropy, and the press
have found the movement to be too much for the old token efforts
and the traditional palliatives. The middle of the road has become
an unsafe and confusing place to stand.

Increase of Self-Confidence Among Young Negroes

Those who have been closest to the youthful freedom-thrust
participants and who have been in a position to observe at first
hand the initial results are compelled to comment on the self-
assurance, the confidence, and the feeling of success that radiated

among these young warriors. At first they were like soldiers returning from a brilliant campaign, or like the football team running off
the field and bouncing off the excess power after a sweeping
homecoming victory.

This was more than a mere adolescent response after a spring
festival, for indeed there had been a great moral triumph. America
had been brought to a moment of truth. Thoughtful people stood
dazed at seeing an irreversible process in history having its incep-
tion before their very eyes. In southern towns secretaries, janitors,
merchants, and shoppers looked down from their Main Street,
second and third floor barricades, watching the young Negroes
march through southern cities around the bases of monuments of
Confederate generals mounted on trusty steeds. As they watched,
their jaws sagged with shock and passiveness, and their eyes were
like glass. They could not believe what they saw. Those youngsters
whom they thought to be happy-go-lucky, generally stupid, care-
free, docile, and fearful, were jamming up the traffic arteries and
defying the verdict of the centuries which had indicted them as
inferior beings, incapable of such a determined course of action.

It was no petty success, for they knew that they were right, and
the sheer happiness that they discovered in their demonstrations bore
adequate evidence for them that there was more fulfillment to be
found in this than in any other option that lay before them. In
addition to a very mature moral assessment of the issues, they had
the added impetus of the youthful requirement to break with
tradition, to defy adult sanctions, and to go on their own. They
were on stage, and the entire world was their audience. Young
people everywhere need to be moving. They must see the passing
scene swiftly approaching and departing. They need to elbow their
way through the maze of inherited values and practices, and stand
on their own threshold of history. The young Negro is no exception, and the awareness that this had been accomplished was the
most obvious result of the take-over by the young.

It is understandable that a measure of arrogance was the
corollary to this victory. It was forgivable, but it must not be
allowed to go unchallenged. They began to compare their bold
attack on segregation with the slower pace of the major ameliorat-
ing organizations, such as the National Urban League and the
NAACP. They were brashly inclined to sweep these movements off

the record of history with one stroke and paint a picture of themselves as the true emancipators of the Negro. On the contrary, without the legal victories of the NAACP and the establishment of a climate of expectancy, these young people would have found no basis for their assertiveness. Because they lived and acted out their drama largely in the South where there were very few local Urban Leagues, they were not fully aware of the nature of the work of this organization, but much of what they took for granted regarding the inherent equality of the races, their own self-respect, their own preparation for new opportunities, and the justifications for urgent change, represented ideas poured into the stream of American consciousness by the Urban League and its allies.

Their greatest contempt, however, was for the leaders of Negro education, those who lived in the brick houses on the tar surface road, who drove the finest cars and who had the ear of the white power structure. They knew that they had undercut their influence unquestionably; and the smirk of pride on their faces was directed more to their trustees, principals, and presidents, their deans and professors, than to anyone else.

Indeed, there was some justification for this. Many leaders in education had made compromises that were uncalled for. Many of them were enjoying economic and social success, perhaps unwittingly, at the expense of the retardation of the progress of their people toward full emancipation. Nevertheless, this by no means characterized the vast majority of them. Most of these men were born in the midst of all the paraphernalia of a segregated society. They excelled their peers in attaining education. They cultivated personal discipline and had acquired advanced degrees. They had won the respect of both the white community and their Negro confreres.

Because of their perception of the requirements for equality, they carried in their bosoms a burning desire to see young Negroes cultivate a taste for decorum, a sense of personal and racial pride, dedication to the indices of strong character, and a mastery of history, the fine arts, the sciences, and technology as a basis for advancement of the race. Many of the coaches saw new careers emerging and begged on their knees for contracts with professional ball clubs for their athletes. Many of these men had choked down insults before state legislative bodies and had felt their pride walked on by white school boards and superintendents in order to gain an advantage for young Negroes. They were so obsessed with the pursuit of white middle-class standards and the desire to see young Negroes emulate their criteria of culture that they had become blind to the larger issue of a social order that was practically cancelling out their efforts as fast as they could make them. Again, there were moral failures among them and there was cowardice in their ranks, but it is unfair to characterize them generally as selfish compromisers concerned primarily with their own salvation.

The Negro educators of the South were not unlike their counterparts in the North—prosperous preachers, social welfare administrators, city and state "colored firsts," who worked hard for status and income and sought to protect their gains by emulating the manners of their associates and minimizing conflict situations. They did not regard themselves as enemies of racial advance. To the contrary, they saw themselves as the *avant-garde*.

Much of the activity of 1960–1963 centered around the campuses of the small, private, church-founded Negro colleges. These colleges were turned over to Negro presidents during the forties, approximately, and the sponsoring mission boards began to withdraw support at one of the lowest points of the American economy. Many of these new presidents had to go to the local banks and borrow money on their own credit to meet payrolls. They were very lonely men because many people who had never seen their audit sheets and who had no knowledge of their personal indebtedness, felt that they and their institutions were far more secure than they actually were. Without the sacrifices of many of these men, and without their willingness to go begging with their hats in their hands, pleading for an opportunity for the rising Negro generation, the young Negroes would never have been brought to such a level of competence that they could challenge the entire social order. These young people were really too eager to pause and assess the role of the Negro administrator in a segregated order, and, as revolutions go, something is always lost for a greater gain. One obvious loss was the prestige of the top Negro who had scaled the heights under the old system. So, the first reaction to their initial successes was found among the demonstrators themselves, the echo of the songs of victory ringing in their souls, and the wreaths of triumph stacked high on their heads.

Apprehension on the Part of Negro Adults

The second response to the freedom thrust on the part of the young Negro was the scampering of frightened Negro adults looking for cover. In retrospect, one may be certain that many of them are now ashamed of their first reactions. The most nervous ones went to the telephones and confided to their white friends that they had had no part in this. Other intelligentsia sat silently through heated discussions, giving tacit consent to remarks that repudiated the young Negroes. Negro professionals who were deeply in debt and who were determined to hold fast to the priceless private gains that they had made in life, quaked at what might happen when the white community organized for revenge.

An example of the estrangement that developed may be seen in the following typical encounter with the new breed and the old. When the first freedom riders went South they stopped at Greensboro, North Carolina, the city in which the sit-ins began. There was a rally held for them, attended by an audience made up of supporters as well as frightened curiosity seekers. When the meeting was over, a staff member of the local Negro college telephoned its president and informed him that the group was hungry and that most places were closed at that late hour. The president invited all of them to come to the campus College Inn and served them a late snack. James Farmer of CORE was with the group, and he commented to the president that this was altogether unexpected; for he had not imagined that a Negro college president in 1963 would risk his job entertaining freedom riders. This was the general view held by those who were in the vanguard of the movement.

A few days later, after the same bus that had come through Greensboro had been burned, and the freedom riders beaten and left without medical attention, a Negro newsman scurried around Birmingham trying to find treatment for a young Morehouse College student whose head was gashed. Among the Negro physicians whom he found, not one of them felt that he could afford to be involved to the extent of giving medical service to this young freedom rider. Such would not be the case today at all; for the movement has gained acceptance, and nearly every Negro is proud to be identified with it. But in the early stages an undeniable response to this bold freedom thrust was fear on the part of status

Negroes and resultant contempt for them on the part of the young rebels.

A companion point is that the Negro community quickly divided: those who did applaud the movement, on the one hand, and those who decried it, on the other. It was difficult to stand in the middle because constant discussion and debate finally pushed every Negro to one side or another of this issue. Of course, this first general reaction of fear and apprehension on the part of Negroes who had much to lose did not last. Many of them finally came to the other side and gave support to the entire movement; others were honestly discriminating and gave consent to some phases of it though disapproving others.

It is not true that all Negro professionals felt the threat of the loss of their jobs, for many of them were sophisticated enough to know that white professionals were not ready to take on the indelicacy of teaching Negroes, or the tasks of performing medical, dental, or even mortuary services and assuming other professional responsibilities for Negroes. There was in reality never any danger of liquidating Negro professionals.

Exposure of White Hatemongers

The third reaction is the one best known, the uncovering of the naked animosity of white hate groups. It is interesting, however, that the young Negro has never paused to give serious consideration to these groups, and he has not yet assessed the support that these groups received from respected whites. He saw this as a development among poor, uneducated whites who had no status in town, who could inflict violence as their only weapon, and who were therefore no major threat to them. They were convinced that decisions regarding integration would be made downtown by the college-bred businessmen, from the old families who were Episcopalians and Presbyterians, and who told poor whites what to think and what to do in the long run. These hate groups had already begun to grow following the 1954 decision and the Little Rock incident. The young Negroes had heard their conversations around the feed stores, filling stations, and bus terminals. They had heard the whining apostles of Hargis and McIntyre parroting themes about law and order, old-fashioned patriotism, Communists under pillows and behind draperies, and stirring up the uninitiated with a steady vibration of white supremacy and begging from them prayers and checks.

They knew that this ground swell of hatred would influence elections and cause moderate Southerners to lose office, but they saw this as a phase of the total process and nothing to be excited about. They were attacking the entire system, and the minor details regarding which segregationist won the State House did not impress them.

It is doubted, however, that they anticipated the measure of violence and the extremes to which some of these hatemongers would go. Perhaps no one really envisaged the burning of scores of churches and the cowardly and random murder of Negroes like Lemuel Penn from ambush on the open highways. The treatment that the early demonstrators received at the hands of the local police gave them reason to feel that at least there would be minimal protection against the loss of life and limb at the hands of white mobs.

When the families of civil rights martyrs Michael Schwerner and James Chaney asked their attorneys to schedule an autopsy, the best pathologist available was sought. The bodies of these two young civil rights workers, along with Andrew Goodman, lay on a slab in a Mississippi morgue, offered up, like countless others, on the altar of racial justice. In this struggle for a real breakthrough in the impenetrable deep South, it will probably require many more bodies lying in morgues waiting for unwelcomed family physicians to add another word of corroboration that it was indeed as brutal as the papers said it was. The autopsy revealed that there was really no limit to the cruelty that white vengeance was capable of delivering.

Dr. Charles Goodrich, one of the top medical men of the country, had joined Dr. Aaron O. Wells, a popular and talented New York internist, in a volunteer service sponsored by the Medical Committee on Human Rights. Dr. Goodrich got in touch with the expert pathologist, Dr. David Spain, at his summer place on Martha's Vineyard. Goodrich and Spain arranged to strain the airline schedules, their luck held out, and they succeeded in getting together in Jackson with Wells.

The narrative of this "operation autopsy" moves with goose-pimpled intensity, like a drawn-out escape from Dachau. These determined physicians had resolved to stay soul-deep in the midst of this blood-curdling investigation. Jack Pratt, a computer-brained, selfless white civil rights lawyer, was the mentor. He had played tag with legal head hunters in Mississippi to get a post-mortem. All else failing, the Chaney family arranged to have their son's body released to them and the autopsy would follow. The doctors were harassed by every test of endurance and, in addition to their own composure to worry about, they had to lend courage to the Negro undertaker who was understandably nervous about his future.

With all the delaying tactics, and with pounds of paper and hours of telephone mischief behind them, Wells, Goodrich, and Pratt finally had Spain on his way to the University of Mississippi Medical Center.

Spain was first struck by the fact that Chaney was a small boy. He could hardly stop anyone from brutalizing his frail frame. His wrist was broken to a flapping state, his jawbone was split, his right shoulder was crushed, his skull was crushed also. Dr. Spain said: ". . . he must have been beaten with chains or a pipe. . . . I could barely believe the destruction to these frail young bones. In my twenty-five years as a pathologist and medical examiner, I have never seen bones so severely shattered, except in tremendously high-speed accidents or airplane crashes. It was obvious to any first-year medical student that this boy had been beaten to a pulp." This must be counted among the fast-moving events in the wake of the young Negroes' drive for rapid changes. The curtain was drawn back on this monstrous hate mentality that has horrified the world.

Certainly no one was prepared to hear from white Northerners the hue and cry about "law and order." Negroes in the South who were not familiar with the details of white communities had been led to accept the view that Yankees were generally callous to the plight of southern Negroes but certainly not hostile toward them. The young Negro, although surprised by this crescendo of letters from northern readers to northern editors, recognized it as the voice of the enemy of their cause and gave no credence or validity to the claims that the preservation of law and order in matters like the movement of traffic was more important than the demonstrations the Negroes felt were necessary for justice and full citizenship.

Support from White Liberals

The fourth reaction was consternation among the tea-and-cookie white liberals—not the genuine liberals—who deplored the Negroes' plight but who were always ambivalent, straddling the thin line between a conscience that called for decency and the atavistic drag on human nature that called for social inertia and self-preservation. Most white liberals saw the emancipation of the Negro as something inevitable in American life, but it was like the coming of springtime, something that would be brought about without too much direct effort on their part, although with their entire approval. Indeed, there were exceptions. There were those like Sarah Patton Boyle, of Charlottesville, whose courage, strength, and transparency are like tulips growing in the snow.

Among the most heartening responses has been the consolidation of the already enlightened position of women's groups. Somehow men have been robbed of their social sensitivity by their obsession with careers and money. While they have been choking down sandwiches at the desk between frantic telephone calls their wives have been distilling refreshing ideas about the destiny of the human family. Perhaps also it is the maternalism in women that causes them to have a more highly developed capacity for vicarious experiences and purely altruistic motivation. Nonetheless, the young Negro is heavily indebted to the League of Women Voters, the Young Women's Christian Association, the united women's groups representing Catholic, Protestant and Jewish faiths, the organizations of college and university women, and the leadership that individual women give to other organizations. Of course, the support of the Negro women's organizations under Dorothy Height was expected and it has been a steady, strong arm of the entire effort.

At the same time, young Negroes were disappointed at the support they received from intellectual Jews living in the South. Many of the department stores against which the demonstrations were directed were owned and managed by very sophisticated Jews. In terms of the kinds of sermons that rabbis had been preaching and the deluge of liberal literature pouring out of Jewish organizations based in New York, the Negroes had a right to expect more support than they received. To their amazement, they discovered that the Jewish community identified with the white

South and, therefore, sided against the young Negroes. Jewish businessmen in Montgomery, Alabama, and in Albany, Georgia, backed their brave rabbis against the wall and made them squirm for the freedom to echo the voice of the prophet Amos who said, "But let justice roll down like waters and righteousness like an everflowing stream." Many rabbis were heroes of this movement, but young Negroes still could not understand why Jewish laymen in the South were so indifferent to Negro success in social change.

The Jewish community knew that their situation in the South was at best tenuous. Jews had only ceremonial social contact with the white South. They lived on a cultural island that gave them no security when the floods descended and the gales of change began to blow. Intellectually they were bound to understand the Negro's desire to break the walls of the ghetto and to move into America's mainstream. But they were not secure enough in these communities to risk their privileges in the Negro's behalf. It is rash, however, to say that the Jews of the South were indifferent. It is fairer to say they felt that this was not their business and that they had nothing to gain by getting involved in a battle between black and white Christians, taking sides in a dispute in which they felt they had no stake at all.

Another development that accompanied the emergence of the young Negro was the surfacing of concern on the part of thousands of articulate, courageous and unflagging white students and volunteers. These zealous freedom fighters left their shrubbed suburbs, Gothic campuses and weekend parties to wade out into the mainstream of civil rights activity, a long way from the shallows of split-level America's superficial pursuit of tinseled status symbols. They were ridiculed by friends, abandoned by peer groups, read out of the family by grandparents, scratched off the mailing lists of young lovers and branded as a part of the neurotic, adventurous "left."

Many of them did more than take a weekend excursion to Selma, Birmingham or Greenville. They are in the South now. They are still in Harlem and Syracuse. They are a part of the struggle for keeps. They have cast their lot. They have a new selfhood.

The Peace Corps likewise magnetized large numbers of this new breed who were ready for challenges of new moral dimensions. They saw in the faces of little Nigerian boys and girls the traces of our common humanity; they stayed close enough to the people to penetrate the veneer of cultural variety and to discover the abiding human continuum that makes the seas seem narrow and the mountains like level places.

These new apostles of the day have the advantage of knowing that at any moment they can retrace their steps and revert to the white majority to assume business as usual. This may tend to discount the earnestness of their effort, but before this conclusion is drawn, the value of even a brief exposure to life from another perspective must not be denied. Before an appreciable number of political, educational and government leaders can be found who will know enough about the human problems without depending upon vicarious reflections, there needs to be a larger delegation from the secure, affluent strata making common cause with the deprived people of the world.

The young Negro must be credited with the achievement of placing a new premium upon the early break in normal career schedules and the acknowledgment of "extra-career" and "extra-class" involvement in social change as a necessary corollary to a sane estimation of the world's need.

There is hardly any name invented, any vulgar epithet in use that has not been hurled at civil rights workers. They have endured every measure of violence and abuse. Their firsthand knowledge of race hatred and resistance to change will surely seep into the public conscience, remold some career plans, give momentum to new organizations and, eventually, influence legislation and jurisprudence.

In fact, the only white people in America who really know what is happening today are those who have leaped clear of the entire structure of the approved, "brand name" culture and roamed off into the forests and underbrush of black discontent.

They know the full measure of contempt the black masses have for "Anglo-Saxon" Negroes. They have heard the name calling, the snide remarks and the shouts of condemnation.

They have seen the yawning vacuum of leadership created by the swish of college bred Negroes chasing each other for the trophies of white approbation. For days and months they have gone in and out of the hollows of the rural South and the dungeons of the urban North wondering where the "top" Negroes were.

They have seen the rubble of twisted humanity lying wasted around the bars in the cities and the filling stations in the countryside. They have heard their jokes, songs, moans and sighs bespeaking despair and hopelessness.

They have been abused by the red-neck white as a "nigger-lover" and condemned by the intellectual black militant as a dangerous, paternalistic subverter of black integrity, a pawn of white liberalism to check the tide of black anger.

They have seen the black-suited, Cadillac-addicted, cigar-chewing downtowners ignore the new black mood as the temporary rumbling of a few erratic fellows with beards who are too slick to work. They have been ushered out of one office after another as they tried to convey the message that time is running out.

They have seen so much that no one will believe and it is this dilemma that presages a longer-term one, namely: How can the power structure be awakened to the urgency of renovating the system to include a program that spells hope for the Negroes before it is too late and no Negro can be found willing to talk?

Deepening of the Chasm Between White Christians

The fifth reaction to the sudden burst of activity on the part of the young Negro was the deepening of the chasm between white Christians. The Catholics came off better than the Protestants in this matter. They had the advantage of a hierarchical system and a long tradition of obedience to their spiritual leaders. Men like Bishop Waters of the Raleigh, North Carolina, diocese did not play with this issue. A dissident segregationist group in Louisana even drew the penalty of excommunication. With the possible exception of the Negro Catholics in Louisiana, their numbers in the South are so scattered that a comparison between Catholic response and Protestant reaction requires further discussion, and the mere announcement of statistics and proclamations will not suffice.

The South is Protestant. It is largely made up of Baptists, Methodists, and Presbyterians, with a fair number of Episcopalians among the privileged classes and smaller Pentecostal and Fundamentalists groups among the lowest economic classes. One has to be very careful in making glib observations regarding church people, for these people who populate the churches are the same people who populate the factories, the businesses, the service clubs, and the American Legion Posts. They arrive at their value structure in an eclectic fashion, taking some from the preaching of the gospel and some from a value system based on empirical deductions from participation in the culture. Thus, when white ushers stand at the front door and bar Negroes from attending a worship service they do not consider that they are violating the teachings of the spirit of Christ. On the contrary, they are being obedient to another sanction in their value structure, the mores of the white South, which dictate that Negroes should not sit on soft cushions in an air-conditioned building and sing the Lord's praises with a voice equal to their own. Not even this form of equality can be conferred, no matter what the gospel says. They rationalize that the Negroes would have been welcomed had they come in the spirit of worship, but everyone knows that the Negroes would not have been welcomed so long as their faces were black.

Much of this has changed. Many preachers have been able to work their way out of this by tenaciously upholding the principles of the Christian faith in the face of great opposition. It is no simple matter for a Protestant pastor to stand against the opinions of the majority of his congregation; for although the rhetoric of the sermon says that the Lord planted him there, the members recollect all too well the night that they voted to call him rather than someone else. It was a somewhat cool-headed evaluation that brought him rather than another minister. They may refer to the Gothic edifice as the house of the Lord, but they remember all too well the arguments with the architect, the negotiations with the bank, and the long nights of planning on how to meet the mortgage payment. So, there is a very real conflict between what they understand to be the injunctions of Micah and Amos and what they feel is an obligation to themselves. Nevertheless, the young Negroes drove a wedge into the white Protestant community. The liberal preacher had to give assent to the rightness of their cause and, since he was often supported by persons who respected his moral integrity, the churches divided.

Dr. Robert W. Spike, formerly director of the Commission on Religion and Race of the National Council of Churches, has described the dilemma of the churches as follows:

A real rift developed between the opinions of the better-trained white clergymen and their laymen. The clergymen were appalled by the misunderstanding of propositional theology and the insistence that faith was only a personal matter. These clergymen, and some laymen, grew more and more pessimistic about the role of religion in American life —seeing it increasingly as an ornament, without substantive influence. Strong laymen, on the other hand, often reacted with increasing frustration to the clergymen. Either they deplored the concern of their ministers for public issues and turned to pseudoreligious (the John Birch Society and other far-right organizations are really heretical religious movements), or they despised the church as not being worth bothering about except for ceremonial occasions.[1]

The problem with the Protestant community in the South—and in the North, for that matter—in most small towns, is that the gospel preached to the people is a palatable message on the themes of personal escape from the vicissitudes of this life and victory in the life to come. It is not oriented toward the advent of the kingdom of God in the midst of history. The Protestant social gospel in America had Yankee origins, centered around Colgate-Rochester Divinity School in upstate New York, Union Theological Seminary in New York City, Yale Divinity School, and the seminaries in Chicago. This lack of contact between Christians in the two sections of our country has inhibited the free flowing of new ideas from one part to the other. Because the South has been largely rural and anti-intellectual, urban concepts regarding the renovation of society have had little southern support. The social gospel derives from a broad-gauge understanding of the dealings of God with man in the Bible and the concern to translate the will of God into concrete proposals for the social order. Rural people are more likely to be loyal to the literal, verbal message than to the derivative social teachings and ethical ideas.

This is bound to change as the South becomes more urban and as the gnawing problems of the city cry out for answers. Today there is very little difference between a well-educated Protestant minister of whatever denomination in the South and one in the North. This ecumenizing effect has already taken place to a large extent and it will spread. But when the young Negroes made their onslaught against segregation, they caught the vast multitudes of the southern Protestant community unprepared, and they had to reckon with this issue largely out of the void of an outmoded, conservative, ornamental, irrelevant, credulous biblicism. The radical Jesus of history they had not dealt with, and his teachings were very narrowly interpreted. The love for others that he taught was sublimated beneath his teachings on purity and piety for the individual. Notwithstanding, giants in southern pulpits were able to speak creatively, and they did show the way. Some of them, like Charlie Jones of Chapel Hill, had already paid the price of the loss of his pulpit on this issue before the young Negro emerged as a civil rights leader. And men like Carlyle Marney of Charlotte have been such towering spiritual leaders that their views have had to be respected.

Of course, there is still something spurious about the argument that the radiance of the Christian gospel should have been expected to shine more brightly on the race issue than it had on other matters. The Protestant South had neglected many items of social concern quite apart from the race issue. Again, this is because there was a preoccupation with personal salvation after death rather than an emphasis upon a better way of life for people here and now. The economic plight of the poor white Southerner is as much a reflection of this otherworldly emphasis in religion as is recalcitrance concerning the changing status of the Negro.

The Negro churches of the South—and hence, of the northern ghettos, which represent a direct transplant of southern Negro culture—have the same preoccupation with personal salvation. The young Negroes forced many of their pastors toward a redefinition of the fullest meaning of religious experience. In most of these pulpits God had been portrayed as a cosmic bellhop, rushing favors to those who were patient and persistent in calling upon him, without much emphasis upon the obligation of the Christian to apply the spiritual insights of the Judeo-Christian message to his society. The total moral fiber of the Negro community would be greatly strengthened if the preachers promised a little less on the part of God and demanded a little more on the part of the people.

The civil rights movement was generated outside the churches and then drafted the services of Negro ministers into its leadership; likewise, the response to the civil rights movement is unrelated to church statistics among southern white Christians. If anything, the relationship is an inverse one, showing greatest resistance to change in areas where church statistics are most impressive. Thus, one of the most significant results of the initiative assumed on the part of the young Negro has been the re-examination of the meaning of religion in the Protestant churches of the South.

What is said here about the South applies largely to white churches throughout the country, for increasingly we are coming to understand that on the matter of race the difference is not so much a matter of North or South as it is the density of the Negro population. And concepts regarding the social application of the gospel tend to correspond to the degree of urbanization and the extent of contact with the flow of liberating ideas from the humanities, the social and natural sciences rather than to regions.

Heartening Response by Government, Foundations, Business, and Press

On a more positive note, the sixth response to the emergence of the young Negro as a revolutionary has been very heartening. In government circles, among the major foundations of America, in the business community, and in the national press the cause has been advanced in giant steps. Taking these in reverse order, the press has had a field day on this issue. Only a major war has succeeded in dominating the press as much as the activity of the young Negroes and those movements encouraged by their aggressiveness have done. Television found in this one of the most popular topics that it ever seized upon. One may wonder if the successes of the Negro people would have been possible without the contribution of newsmen who stood eyeball to eyeball with every development, often risking their lives to get a story. The Negro press, happily, has shown itself also to be a continuing, valuable, and integral part of American journalism, for it has often caught an angle overlooked by the major metropolitan dailies and the weekly news magazines. It is interesting that in the stiffest possible competition the Negro press continues to fill a unique role, throwing light into many shadowy corners that are often overlooked by the major media.

Even those newspapers, magazines, and editors like Richmond's Jack Kilpatrick, who fought the Negroes relentlessly, have been very helpful in exposing a point of view that was pervasive and operative but nebulous in its articulation and largely unfamiliar in a formalized way to the Negro mind. Many southern Negroes never really knew what white people thought about them until the editorial writers went to work on the Negro cause and evoked a rash of'letters to the editor. The pictures of state troopers mounted on braying horses, backing Montgomery college girls against a brick wall, armed with whips and cattle prods, did more to convince the world of the extent of hatred inherent in racism than a thousand speeches and books. The coverage given the March on Washington brought this spectacular event into the living room of most American homes.

Any device that could bring America face to face with President Johnson as he spoke following the stampeding of unarmed Negroes in their first attempt to march from Selma to Montgomery— any mechanism that could capture those somber tones of his voice on that occasion and radiate the earnestness of his spirit is a powerful lever for social change. Five minutes of a confrontation such as President Johnson had with the American conscience is worth five years of listening to public speakers with no authority and with no significant power at their command.

Leadership on the part of President Kennedy and President Johnson has moved the American business community off dead center. When one sees a Negro selling tickets behind a counter in the Charlotte airlines terminal he must not believe that this has come about because of a sudden change of heart on the part of the airlines. This is the direct result of initiative from the White House. It was a long time coming, but today all the major corporations of America—with very few exceptions—have committed themselves to a changed policy in the hiring of Negroes. The evidence for this is overwhelming and on every hand. In a meeting with personnel managers, a vice-president of the Radio Corporation of America said that he did not want his men to come back explaining *that they could not find* capable Negroes; he wanted them to come back explaining *how they succeeded* in finding them. He further admonished them to make this only one part of their total commitment to equality. He urged them to be identified in their communities as men of justice and fair play in housing, in recreation and in support of movements working for equal opportunity. This kind of preaching on the part of a corporation vice-president is hopeful indeed. This was not done before the young Negroes began to assert themselves. The problem today, of course, is finding the Negroes who are prepared to take advantage of the opportunities, but before 1960 the problem was finding opportunities that would beckon, inspire, and challenge young Negroes.

There are some who object to the response of business on the grounds that they are overcompensating in giving preferential treatment to Negro applicants. But persons inside the business community know how deliberate and how long the effort has been made to keep Negroes out. They know better than anyone else the justification for a commensurate and deliberate effort, now, to get Negroes in. This is simply a corrective measure, a fair one and well understand by those who want to understand it.

We see all too clearly the reasons for supporting foreign aid programs in Asia, Africa, and Latin America. We tackle the problems of literacy, health, and technology to offset a lag that means both shame and danger to our country. We must see the shame and danger in the incongruities of the Negroes' position in America and take corrective steps.

In an address before the Indiana State Chamber of Commerce in December of 1963, Lawrence E. Laybourne, of *Time,* put it this way:

Not many managers are willing, on purely semantic grounds, to use the word "preference" in this connection. But, whatever the terminology, the spirit of the Pitney-Bowes approach—the determination to try very hard to find Negro candidates for jobs and give them extra help and extra training in making good on those jobs—is shared by an increasing number of companies. A national problem exists, acutely; and good corporate citizenship requires that management make a sustained attempt to contribute to its eventual solution.

Another aspect of the response to the young Negro's initiative has been on the part of the major foundations who for years made only token gestures toward the Negroes. They are now looking for creative ideas that will help to overcome the abuses of the past and establish procedures that will accelerate the advancement of the preparation of young Negroes. Several foundations have even found ways of contributing directly to the civil rights cause in addition to grants for reading programs, experiments in curriculum revision, and in faculty and student exchanges between the Negro colleges of the South and the stronger institutions of the North and South. Scholarship programs and research grants have been enlarged and made more inclusive, and hardly is there a single idea with any possibility for effective implementation that cannot find financial support in the area of upgrading the Negro people. This was not the case before the young Negro began his march. This activity must be attributed to the awakening of the nation's conscience as a sequel to sit-in demonstrations and protest movements.

Nevertheless, neither the American business community nor the foundations can do enough to compensate for the long years of neglect. These segments of American life, which were practically immune to threats and reprisals, can offer little excuse for showing so little concern about the Negro people for so long. One reason that so many Negroes—even with degrees—are not better educated today is that they had no vision of the fruits of education, they saw no future in the world of business and industry. Any discussion of the aspirations of young Negroes must be dealt with in the light of this long delay in presenting to them an invitation to prepare for the tough and demanding assignments at the hub of American industry and commerce. Hardly enough can be done to offset the consequences of neglect that are all about us and that are practically impossible to rectify among those who are in their late teens, no matter how much effort is now put forth. It is gratifying to observe, however, how much brighter the future will be for young Negroes as the foundations and the corporations continue to respond to the challenge to provide equal opportunity.

Negroes have always had to look to the federal government for what little they have received, and when the federal government has failed them, their condition has been most pitiable. Nothing has given so much heart to the Negro's cause, therefore, as the presence of federal troops in Little Rock, the expenditure of nearly a half-million dollars to secure the admission of James Meredith to the University of Mississippi, federal marshals commanding Governor Wallace on the campus of the University of Alabama to move out of the way so that a Negro could register, the appointment of Negroes to highly visible positions in government, and the presence of Negroes at White House affairs. Of course, there is much more to be accomplished, and there are still many areas where lesser federal officials have not kept pace with White House leadership. Nevertheless, this is perhaps the most hopeful of all the responses to the protest movements inaugurated by young Negroes—the awakening of the federal establishment.

What makes the federal involvement so hopeful, and is it desirable to have such a heavy hand of government in these matters? This is an honest question. The answer is that the least amount of government is still the best amount, but how much "least" is must be determined by how much neglect the government must offset. In the matter of Negro progress, not only has the private sector left the Negro out, but much has been done, in the South especially, to defeat him and to cancel out his own meager efforts. Where provincialism and the denial of opportunity affect the destiny of a large segment of the population, and the consequences become a scandal of national proportions, whose business is it if not the government's? Only the federal government can marshal the leadership, make available the money and the power to reduce the effect of discrimination on the part of private business, local and state governments, and voluntary agencies.

Consider the shameful loss of manpower and the sheer human waste created by the thousands of Negroes who cannot get on the job rolls because of lack of adequate educational opportunity. No agency has the resources to tackle this cyclops like the government. In the summer of 1965, for example, the Office of Economic Opportunity granted $2,200,000 to seventeen colleges to work with young people of college potential whose condition of poverty would otherwise reduce their chances of enrolling. The bulk of the money went for summer remedial work to prepare these students for admission and for survival in college. This program is dubbed "Upward Bound."

Included in the spectrum of programs was a grant of $157,000 to Columbia University to reach into neighboring Harlem and lead 160 ninth-graders to a higher plateau of educational performance. Tuskegee Institute had a grant to find 600 students strong enough to tutor 9,900 youngsters in low-income families in eleven Alabama counties. Ripon College in Wisconsin had a grant to provide summer study for thirty Menominee Indian youth. The College of the Ozarks in Arkansas had $41,000 to help eighty students from poverty-ridden homes.

Here we see a sample of the massive effort being made to give respiration to the poor who have been suffocating for years in an atmosphere of limited opportunity. These are not efforts to reward lazy people for their indolence; rather, it is relief to aid them in recovering from deprivations.

The activity of the Justice Department in seeking legal redress for Negroes in voting and in cases of employment discrimination is also an indispensable activity of government. Though specific laws have not been broken in every instance of discrimination, the entire spirit of the Constitution has been made a mockery. The Constitution was meant to give a definition to citizenship, to cancel arbitrary personal advantages and to grant equal protection to every citizen. Thus, the present activity of the government is crucial to the success of the efforts of the Negroes, but it is something new since 1960.

Opponents to extensive federal involvement in the Negro's cause allege that this is nothing more than a bid for the large urban Negro vote. Even so, in terms of goals, if the Negro had to choose between two candidates who were equally indifferent to his interests, the size of his vote would be of little consequence to him. He is very fortunate that he can make his vote count on the federal level. It still means little in many local and state elections.

In the administration of President Johnson, already the Negro people have made more progress than they had made since Reconstruction. It is fortunate for the Negro people, for America, and for the cause of democracy in the world that these two neo-emancipation presidents, Kennedy and Johnson, had the moral stature to respond to the earnestness of the Negro's drive for equality and to respond with affirmative action.

One must speculate on what would have happened had the vigorous young Irish Catholic President lived, whose style of life and whose courage of convictions brought so much hope to the Negro people. There is little question that the pace set by President Johnson will deliver the Negro people to a plateau of civil liberty, economic emancipation, and social equality that not even the young Negroes of 1960 anticipated with their fondest dreams.

When the first Negro college students sat-in at a dime store counter to get a coke and a hot dog, they had no idea that the responses to this action would be so far-reaching. The key to it all is that they followed a technique of peaceful, passive resistance that unlocked a floodgate of moral energy in America. A violent, subversive, seditious movement would have resulted in the insulation of Negroes in a moral no-man's land. But the dignified and sustained nonviolent protest has unprecedented numbers of sincere Americans looking for feasible ways of rectifying a moral failure and erasing its effects.

3

Reversing the Spiral Toward Futility

THUS far we have been talking mainly about the young Negroes from relatively secure backgrounds, those who were enrolled in colleges and who had been in quest of freedom as a consequence of the encouragement of their parents and the expectations of the aspiring communities in which they were reared. The very fact that they manifested such concern for their future and for the future of their people is evidence that they were not trapped at the end of that spiral which had been moving toward futility for thousands of their neighbors and friends.

A Look at High School Dropouts

Before any discussion of the future of the young Negro can get very far, one must turn his attention to the other end of the spectrum and see the half-million or more young Negroes between 16 and 21 who have been called "dropouts." This is really an undetermined quantity, for in addition to the actual dropouts, there are perhaps just as many "drip-outs" who are still on the school rolls, living on their parents, loitering in the halls, smoking in the restrooms, and strolling in and out of classes without pencils, books, or homework. If we are talking about discouraged, disheartened, angry, and hostile young people who are poorly prepared for the jobs that are open, and who feel no throbbing ambition to be "somebody" in life, we are probably talking about a million and a half rather than a mere half-million. For every one of them who may be identified by his appearance, the company he keeps, or his record in the juvenile court, there are at least two more whose condition is the same but whose overt conduct has not brought them to the attention of those who gather statistics.

Our discussion must begin at this ebb tide of wasted lives, for we must talk of the young Negro as a chronological wave rather than as a vertical sampling of several types. At this point in history the difference between one type of young Negro and another is not nearly so instructive as the difference between a boy with a black face and one with a white. We are talking about the nature of the problem of full participation in American life, equal opportunity for a job—not in contrast with another more qualified Negro, but in contrast to a white youth of the same background, the privilege of using a swimming pool, the chance for quality education, encouragement in participating in cultural and recreational programs, and the subtle advantages of moving around without insult and without social symbols of inferior status. This requires us to look at all Negroes growing up in America and reaching their twenties in the early sixties. These young people will be the parents of the young by 1980, and this is the wave that concerns us. And, if the entire age group is before us, those who are lost in futility represent that starting point which is frightening.

The Experience of Rejection

In order to understand what has been happening, one must see the spiraling relationship between those stages of human response that ultimately brought so many young Negroes to their knees in desperation and futility.

The process began with the experience of rejection. It takes very little intelligence for one to observe that he is not wanted in clean, well-appointed places where the best people gather. One soon learns that it means something when the world has a special niche for him, a balcony at the theater, a special day at the county fair, a special seat on a bus, a special door to enter a public facility, a special window at which to stand to buy a hamburger. The entire network of racism serves to entangle one in a web of rejection. Every time he opens his eyes he sees white people in places of privilege and responsibility, driving the state police cars, hostesses on the airlines, clerks in department stores, commentators on the television news programs, and tellers in the banks. The Negroes, his people, are conspicuous for the roles that they play in the community: sweeping, drifting, mopping, driving the trucks, loafing, or performing those chores which require little intelligence and for which the rewards are commensurately low.

The fact of rejection is so self-evident that it takes no demagogue or Communist to remind a young Negro that he is not only rejected, but rejected as a class, as a race. The rejection is obviously not on the ground of personal failure, but on the ground of membership in a rejected group. And every time the young Negro goes out of his door his sense of rejection is reaffirmed. Simeon Booker of *Jet* and *Ebony* summarizes his plight:

Hampered by an insecure parental, financial and cultural background, dwelling in the dingy atmosphere of the ghetto with its accompanying frustration and despair, the Negro faces an uphill battle to become part of the American mainstream. His resources of leadership, finance and strategies are limited. His inspirational symbols are few. The near-poverty status of the Negro virtually presses his nose in the rubble of humanity.[1]

Not only is the deprived Negro rejected by the majority white world; he is rejected by successful Negroes also. After all, the successful Negro has fought so hard to stay clear of this spiral himself that he does not risk being identified with those who are being propelled toward futility. He looks for exclusive relationships that set him apart as a "different kind." He wants to live in a cleaner neighborhood; he wants his children to play with intelligent, good-looking, well-mannered youngsters; he wants to have private parties with polite conversation among his peers, and he is perpetually in flight from those involvements which would tend to confuse him with the deprived Negroes.

When the disadvantaged young Negro moves to the city looking for a way out, there is a committee waiting for him to introduce him to the ways of survival in the urban maelstrom. They take him in, show him the new dances, introduce him to the available girls who are also wallowing in rejection, give him a tour of the bars and the places where "things are happening," and then give him the calling cards of those who will accept him, the nicknames of the persons who have already made an adjustment to futility. When this happens, he is well on his way; for he has found his element and he is among friends.

This young Negro, lost in the labyrinths of futility, will find the city. That is where he finds his own, the "in" crowd with whom he identifies. He needs the support, the comradeship, and the releases that the city affords. But it is not a paradise. Unskilled and unwanted, he finds no haven in the cities. As Harvey Cox, the incisive Harvard social ethicist, observes:

The villager is lured into the city by its noise and neon while at the same time he is pushed out of the village by hunger cramps and empty pockets . . . but he soon discovers that these glittering symbols of freedom and abundance were not fashioned for him. Disillusioned and embittered, he eventually finds his way to the *favela*, the *bidonville*, tar-paper shanty-towns where the world's urban poor huddle together to glare at the affluent world around them and to gnaw on the bones of discontent.[2]

Everything around him seems to suggest that he was correct in assuming his rejected status. The neighborhood in which he must live is dingy, rundown, with high rent for undesirable housing where the health department, the police, and the welfare workers drive or walk through in routine nonchalance leaving things as they are. He does not see much to convince him that the world is trying to change his condition and elevate him to worthwhile pursuits. Thus the spiral begins to move toward futility when one becomes aware that he is a rejected human being.

The depth of the problem of rejection is so hidden that many well-meaning whites miss it. They still look into the Negro world from the outside and prescribe improvements that amount to mild sedatives. They do not grasp at all the point that so long as that Negro world is separated—over there, downtown, uptown, yonder —so long as it is an island where suffering is compounded, where crime breeds, where skin color alone is the badge of residence, where poverty can settle down and do its worst to people, where there is no real escape, where an entire neighborhood is reserved for the "colored"—so long as it stands for the presumption that Negroes belong apart, it spells rejection, loud and clear.

But, the most common sedative used is a new housing project.

James Baldwin, speaking of housing projects for Negroes, says this:

The projects in Harlem are hated. They are hated almost as much as policemen, and this is saying a great deal. And they are hated for the same reason: both reveal, unbearably, the real attitude of the white world, no matter how many liberal speeches are made, no matter how many lofty editorials are written, no matter how many civil-rights commissions are set up. The projects are hideous, of course, there being a law, apparently respected throughout the world, that popular housing shall be as cheerless as a prison. They are lumped all over Harlem, colorless, bleak, high, and revolting. The wide windows look out on Harlem's invincible and indescribable squalor: The Park Avenue railroad tracks, around which, about forty years ago, the present dark community began; the unrehabilitated houses, bowed down, it would seem, under the great weight of frustration and bitterness they contain; the dark, the ominous schoolhouses from which the child may emerge maimed, blinded, hooked, or enraged for life; and the churches, churches, block upon block of churches, niched in the walls like cannon in the walls of a fortress.[3]

What appears to be a sparkling, new beginning is really like a new jail as long as it stands for separateness and, hence, exclusion and rejection.

Rejection moves to fear. Fear is the automatic response that the ego requires when it is threatened, when it is vetoed, thwarted, or suppressed with no escape. This rejected young Negro wears the mask of bravery and Spartan-like courage, but he is really very frightened. He is afraid of big words, afraid of polite company, afraid of large, clean rooms, afraid of printed tests, afraid of the presence of successful people, afraid of those in authority, and afraid of being left alone to examine his life. Observe that he stays in the street and among those people who demand nothing of him but who take him as he is.

A white person, who remains in the matrix of the white world, will never know how this fear is likened to the feeling of extermination and slow death unless he cuts the umbilical cord of contact with the white world and surrounds himself with black faces exclusively for a month or so. Peace Corps volunteers in Africa sometimes experience this exchange of worlds. One said to his director in Nigeria, when he came to Lagos after a month or so at his school in a village of few whites, "I got a shock every time I shaved. My face looked so pale! I felt anemic." This changing of worlds makes clear how far one can be removed from those who may be a few blocks away but really seas apart if the wall of color separates them.

Don Crider, a Baptist missionary who spent his time in the Chin hills of Burma, greeted a Negro visitor from America with these words after months among those who had round, dark, Mongolian faces and who spoke a dialect completely strange to the western ear: "Gee, it is sure good to see a *white* face again." He saw no *white face,* but he heard a *white accent,* bringing him momentarily back to his native Altoona, Pennsylvania, reidentifying himself with the world of his birth, his rearing, his values, his flights of joy, and his nights of restless anxiety.

On the other hand, color is not in itself a sufficient index of cultural homogeneity. In America it is usually the principal line of demarcation. But when a morally sensitive white transcends the mischief of race, he can be made to feel like a stranger among whites.

A white minister who went to Mississippi in the summer of 1964 to work with the ministers, priests, and rabbis during that long, hot summer, found himself, while in Mississippi, more at home with the black population than he did with the whites. The whole value structure that had nurtured his life as a Christian was more to be found with the Negro community in 1964. He said: "It was a strange experience: for the first time in my life I was afraid to be among whites. When I was growing up I always felt uncomfortable when I found myself in the ghetto in St. Louis. Here I found myself always anxious to be back with friends in the Negro community."[4]

Such an experience, rarely encountered by most persons, is a taste of what it can mean to be locked in behind the color wall, feeling not only the distance that exclusion implies but, further, feeling the unquestioned effects of discrimination aimed at all those trapped behind that wall. This is when fear is born. When the whole world seems to be one high wall of enmity, one is driven to fear, an ineffable loneliness even in a crowd. And all sorts of tricks are played on the mind to disguise the crumbling of the ego.

One has to be very close to the private lives of the rejected Negroes to see this element of fear as it is unmasked in new confrontations at the rehearsal stage. Bernstein, in *Youth on the Streets*,[5] reports on a trip involving several tough-talking Philadelphia youngsters going to a beach party in Atlantic City. When they arrived they stayed in the cars until the beach was empty; then they went running into the water with their clothes on. They were not about to expose themselves to the beach crowd, strangers whose manners and whose language they could not understand. They were not accustomed to beaches and they were not going to become a spectacle before those who were more familiar with proper movements on a waterfront. Every way they turn they discover that there are rules, customs, practices, and ways of doing things that are unfamiliar to them.

Not only in the urban North is the young Negro blinded by the glaring signs of rejection, but even the most unsophisticated rural Negro, for example, knows that the "colored" agricultural agents were housed in a building in the "colored" section, away from the decision-making hallway encounters, cafeteria conversations, out of contact with the visiting "experts" and receiving his information distilled through local hands at briefing sessions and on cold, unanalyzed bulletins. The Negro agent was taken seriously in very marginal matters, not on the big issues affecting the long-term poverty of the Negro farmer. This was obvious to all, and was evidence that race alone, rather than other factors like poor education, meant exclusion.

Pursuing this one step further, 92 per cent of Negro farmers still scratch the ground to raise cotton, tobacco, and peanuts mainly and have their fortunes tied to the fluctuations in these markets; on the other hand, the white farmers with the "tender, loving care" of the agricultural hierarchy have received good loans, modernized their farms, diversified their crops, conserved their soil, and kept themselves at a safe margin away from poverty. As early as 1959 less than half of the whites were tied to the cotton, tobacco, and peanut markets exclusively.

Negroes see the farms and the houses and the children, and compare. They visit the lily-white State Department of Agriculture and notice the absence of Negroes, except the one on the elevator and the janitor. They see the second-floor, walk-up, dimly lighted office of the Negro agriculture agent, or even his better-appointed office on the Negro state college campus, securely distant from the flow of information at the main office.

This becomes a permanent, visible, and effective sign of rejection; and, because it has such a direct bearing on what one can do for his family, how much preparation one can make for declining years, and how near one stands to the edge of extinction, this rejection implies fear as a habit of mind. If one's forward movement is frustrated and he is impeded in constructive endeavors, he will register his sense of being in some way or another. As naturally as the tide presses toward the shore twice in twenty-four hours, birds take to flight, and rivers course their ways toward the seas, human personalities want to be counted, recognized, and identified.

The Wearying State of Fear

Fear is a wearying state. It soon brings on moral fatigue; and when it cannot resolve itself in constructive, restorative activity, it resigns a person to hostility. America pays a very heavy price for this hostility that it has permitted to congeal in the hearts of the rejected young Negroes. Persons incapable of empathizing with these rejected youngsters say all kinds of silly, irresponsible things about them. They want to attribute their condition to some congenital bestiality about the black people of the world or some inexplicable, psychopathic malady. There is too much evidence on the other side to show that those Negroes whose lives were fed and nurtured by other influences have managed to cope with America's opportunities and challenges successfully without the burden of antiwhite hatreds. Just as the correlation between crime and lack of opportunity is overwhelmingly evident, only the most naïve observers attach a racial cause to chronic hostile behavior. It is the result of rejection and fear.

As one examines the circumstances in which these youngsters grew up, the surprise is not in the prevailing extent of their antisocial behavior but in the fact that there is not more of it. If one wished to design a kind of environment for the purpose of breeding social deviates, indurate criminals, and hostile, perverted human personalities, he could not accomplish it more effectively than to create the bleak circumstances of a filthy Negro slum in one of our country's big cities. For it is through the corridors of pain and poverty in such a ghetto that the spiral moves from rejection, to fear, to hostility, and on to its logical extremity at the point of absolute futility and aimlessness.

This futility stage is not a static condition. The fabric of Negro society is woven from such a miscellany of factors. The family and other institutions have such a fragile structure, reflecting economic fluctuations and mobility, that many Negroes find themselves shuttling precariously along the edge of this futility—those who have not yet been swallowed by it. This is primarily because they cannot move freely in the job market: any day, anywhere a young Negro has a door quietly closed behind him as he is ushered back into the hallway denied employment. Then, even when he is hired and made a member, he is embarrassingly aware of the effort that whites must make to relate to him. And, understandably, his awareness of this effort builds a wall of self-exclusion. Thus, while in the same room, at the next desk, on the same beach, on the same team, with every external requirement for equality satisfied, the warm feeling of being an insider is not easily attained. One then becomes ambivalent about integration. He wonders if it will ever work as long as a black face serves to call up to the threshold of a white man's consciousness all the myths and fables, statistics and jokes that have saturated his mind to make him pity a Negro in trouble, resent one changing his status, laugh with one who is mirthful, and avoid all the rest.

A Negro secretary, engineer, or physician goes to Chevy Chase or Bronxville, Great Neck or Chestnut Hills, looking for that apartment or split-level advertised in the paper. When he approaches the agent or the owner he knows that his glands had better be ready to exude those ego-restoring secretions, for he is really expecting to be turned down in one way or another and shoved back into that faceless mass still crawling slowly out of the slave status even though dressed well, good-looking, degreed, and driving a Lincoln.

Thus, the futility stage is one for which any Negro is a perpetual candidate, for all of them who can read and feel know that they have to tread easy and feel their way in order to avoid falling into the abyss of futility. A Negro who does well in life can never feel that such luck will always accompany his days and he wonders how he could adjust to a brand-new beginning with the odds so heavily against him.

The Young Negro in Desperation

Our concern here, however, is with the desperate young Negro, born since 1940. Those who seek to establish contact find him often about as unresponsive and as uncompromising as a Persian kitten. There is with him an absolute discontinuity about his life. He suspects everyone of being his enemy and he has no confidence in the "do good" programs that seek to reach him. He is not simply mad at whites: he is mad at the present world. For example, Bernstein reported on one large city in terms of violence of persons against persons. The incidents of Negroes against Caucasians was 147. The incidents of bitter Negroes against Negroes was 220. Thus, no one escapes his wrath, and whites alone are not the object of his hatred.

Actually, it may be inaccurate to call this emotion hatred because it is deeper than that. Hatred is directed against a responding being, and at the core of hatred is the desire to see awareness of a wound, a hurt, or an insult by the hated one. Hatred implies injury, not extinction; animus, not destruction.

The young Negro who is aware of being trapped in an endless chasm of futility has already killed the forces that put him there in his mind. And only the frail and tenuous circumstances of family ties, inhibitions about long jail terms, and a little love of intermittent fun with comrades prevent him from actualizing what is already real in his mind. He has slaughtered "big Negroes" by the thousands: preachers, politicians, judges, administrators, Presidential appointees, Congressmen, and chairmen of charitable committees appointed by whites downtown. Big name entertainers, athletes, and civil rights leaders are spared until they join the banquet circuit and start making speeches in downtown hotels wearing tuxedos. And that happens before very long!

In a sense, this crowd is slaughtered first because it is the view of the angry young Negro that it is more ignominious. The view of the angry young Negro is that these black men could not have ascended such heights without selling out the interests of the race to whites at some point. Moreover, if their relationship to black destiny had been sound and proper, they could not possibly hold on to status, for timid Negroes and practically all whites would despise them. So, the middle-class status, ipso facto, is self-condemning. It is regarded as a dishonorable achievement and those who reach it have forfeited the right to exist. Those who debate this point, as the argument goes, merely reveal the extent to which their intelligence has been galvanized by white abstractions. The whites are regarded as unfit to live because they are tied to a cosmic conspiracy, by blood and history, by instinct and by deceitful maneuvers in every language, every age, and under every religion and political nomenclature. The only relationship possible between a sane and perceptive black man and a white is a sustained, mutual exploitation. The angry young Negro accepts only one relationship to whites, and that is an arrangement by which some of the interest on three hundred and fifty years of slave labor can trickle into black hands.

Even though there is no clear or cogent answer to the long-term economic, political, and social issues, there is no doubt in the mind of the angry young Negro that nothing can be done with whites in charge.

This attitude is not very difficult for a young Negro to come by, for at some time or another every Negro must confess that this mood sweeps through his being. But for most, by far, it is ephemeral. They have contacts with whites who defy the generalized ethnic characterization; they see events in world and national history that point to a rising new plateau of freedom, there is the occasional retrospective glance which does indeed reflect hopeful movement and shows some solid gains. Furthermore, there is the conviction that the sure way home in America is right straight through the maze of the dominant white culture, not on its periphery but as a part of its redoing and reshaping, participating in the formation of a new American personality that includes the spirit and presence of the black man as part of the total—integrated like the Jews, the Italians, the Poles, the Scots, and the Swedes—with a self-fulfilling rather than a self-rejecting role. It is this challenge which stiffens the resolve and gives purpose and meaning to the struggles of most Negroes. They have written off the position of racial chauvinism, white and black, as morally untenable, politically self-defeating, historically ill-timed and psychologically a temporizing tranquillity. They do not see any feasibility or any long-run success in widening the racial wall. It is trading one futility for another. It is swinging the pendulum all the way from a justifiable disgust at white failure to a visionary embrace of a black utopia.

Yet, who cannot understand this? How long could America indulge in the debilitating, demoralizing habits of racial injustice without being brought to this pathology of a cancerous, vindictive black reaction to balance out the social chemistry? The young Negro is pinned against the wall of futility where the spiral has pressed him in irreversible stages from rejection through fear and hostility.

Moreover, he continues to see evidence in the press that his attitude of defiance is warranted. The daily paper shows a picture of a man in a police uniform holding a vicious dog while the animal chews on a Negro boy in Birmingham. Another picture shows a policeman clubbing a young Negro in a demonstration. All this confirms his feeling of vindictiveness. He reads about Negroes who have attempted to vote, having their credit cut off, their bank loans recalled, their children intimidated, their churches burned, and their leadership shot in cold blood; while the known assailant is set free by a jury of his moral and social peers.

Anywhere the young Negro is likely to be sworn at, cursed, and condemned; for his circle of work and travel revolves around whites who are vocal about hating Negroes, Jews, and "foreigners." On toilet walls and subway entrances and on the scornful faces of his fellow downtown pedestrians he reads the message. Often he finds a tract comparing him with an ape, or a poorly written letter that scribbles contempt for him in large print and misspelled words. He frequently hears a gravel-voiced evangelist playing havoc with the Bible, making God a founder of the Ku Klux Klan and quoting the Scriptures out of context with a barbarous emasculation of that sublime spiritual witness.

Martin Luther King shared a letter that he received during the Montgomery boycott which read as follows: "You niggers are getting your self in a bad place. The Bible is strong for segregation as of the jews concerning other races [sic]. It is even segregation between the 12 tribes of Israel. We need and will have a Hitler to get our country straightened out."[6]

This is the rot that the young Negro feeds on, and he sinks deeper and deeper into frustration. Thus, is it any wonder that so many of them resign from society and amuse themselves in fighting, drinking, sexual abuse, dope addiction, looting, rioting, and holding every aspect of civil society in great contempt, on the one hand, or resort to the psychological refuge of racial chauvinism?

This is the end of the spiral at the point of abject futility.

The Result of an American Process

Any discussion of the young Negro must include a careful examination of such young people, for they belong to America; they are the result of an American process and they are here to stay. They cannot be wished out of existence, for they are real, living, kicking, breathing persons found in growing numbers in all our urban complexes.

Those who are horrified at the violence and devastation of the recent summer riots in the Northeast and in Los Angeles should reflect upon the meaning of futility. In America, futility devolves rapidly into hostility because one feels robbed, tricked, duped, and exploited. A Negro teen-ager caged in a slum, going to a dirty school, turned down by the apprentice program in the unions, insulted by bored and indifferent teachers, snarled at by big, white policemen, and enveloped in a fog of resignation is not so dazed that he fails to observe the passing parade of white people, who move laterally without impediment in the society and who enjoy all its benefits vertically up and down the economic escalator in response to their initiative and to every ambitious impulse. The riot is the unplanned, unscheduled, spontaneous sputtering of indignation and anger aimed at the whole wide world. It is a corporate response that each one would have made individually if he had had any assurance that he would not be shot in a corner like a crazed dog. But when that single incident occurs it lights the fuse, and the individual becomes a part of a conflagration without any effort at all. A riot is the culmination of a community of feeling, the result of a consensus already arrived at, simply waiting for action.

What can be done to put this spiral into reverse and send it moving in the other direction? It has been moving from rejection, through fear and hostility, and then on to futility. What can send it the other way toward acceptance, confidence and self-esteem, participation, and on to success and self-realization? Before we can begin to discuss what should be done for the already aspiring Negro who is aware of his condition and who is right now seeking ways to alter his way of life, we must deal with the cold fact of the existence of the hundreds of thousands of them who are lost in futility.

What is most unfortunate is that even Negro leadership itself tends to label those youngsters as hoodlums and dismiss them as an embarrassment to the race. More time is spent in describing and castigating them than is spent in seeking ways to reverse the spiral which has delivered them to their plight. And no matter how successful the civil rights victories may be, the Negro people cannot rise very far while being weighted down with this heavy load of deprived persons on the bottom. It is far more attractive to a middle-class Negro leader to continue to move in polite circles among cocktailing whites and his own affluent Negro peers than it is to risk losing his image by identifying himself with the lower classes among his own people. Far too many do not see this slum and its population as a laboratory for testing creative and iconoclastic ideas. They see it as a jungle to be avoided. Yet every major move that the Negroes seek to make must at first fly into the face of a blinding barrage of bad statistics on the hordes of deprived youngsters who are aground in the backwaters of futility.

The factors that complicate the situation are myriad. One element is the real difficulty that these young people face in getting an ordinary job. Our economy and our job market cry for highly trained people. Every effort that they make to find employment bogs down when a high school diploma is required. They are frightened in the first instance when a sophisticated application form is placed before them, and they resent being thoroughly humiliated by their poor handwriting and bad spelling.

Programs to Generate Hope

As one answer to this enigma, Whitney Young, the Urban League chief, has called for a kind of domestic Marshall Plan for Negroes. He argues that Western Europe staggered out of its postwar chaos with a multibillion dollar assist from the United States. In twenty years they came from smoking rubble, millions of dead young fathers, toppled cathedrals, political confusion, monetary play-money, and gutted factories all the way to high-speed expressways, medical research discoveries, and to new, red leather seats at all of the mahogany tables around which the great and powerful sit. Was this the magic of Caucasian genius? Partly. But without the billions shoveled in by Washington, let us say, it would have taken much longer.

The Negro problem is not an exact parallel, but a close enough comparison to suggest the same solution, a big investment of brains, concern, and money. It will take an effort more massive than the present billion-and-a-half experimental war on poverty.

Vice-President Hubert H. Humphrey, in his book entitled *War on Poverty*[7] shows what the TVA did for a region. That area of the country, once barren and dry, is now lush and prosperous. It lies next door to the poorest colony of whites in America who have no TVA! The call for a dramatic, national program has this marvelous precedent.

In TVA territory there is flood control, inexpensive electric power, erosion control, and reforestation. A quarter of a million homes have been blessed by this giant project. Thirty-five new factories in the region have expansion plans with 3,000 new jobs. In the 200-county area, twenty-seven new industries began in 1962 using forest products. This resulted from a deliberate, painstaking focus on a national disgrace with fantastic results.

It may be that the present programs in the Higher Education Act of 1965 and the Economic Opportunity Act of 1964 constitute a beginning of all that we know to do, but just as the TVA is a marvel of *regional economic development,* in the name of God and country we need to match the young Negroes' impatience and expectation with a marvel of *national human development.*

The spiral begins to reverse itself with procedures and programs, however small, or large, that signify to these young people that they are wanted and that they are accepted as persons. The great challenge to education and social work agencies is the need to produce persons who can approach these youngsters without sentimentality, without condescension, but with firmness and a vicarious attitude that inspires confidence.

There is a teacher of girls in one of the roughest junior high schools in North Philadelphia who keeps her home crowded with these teen-agers after school. Her school is a special education institution where youngsters are referred who have been in difficulty and who for many other reasons are best served by this type of homogeneous grouping. What do they do at her home? Well, they go off in groups to rummage sales, purchase old coats, bring them back to the house, and then design new styles for them and go to work remodeling them. They light up like daybreak when they see what they have been able to do with something thrown away. It is as though they were working on their own lives like clay in the potter's hands, melted, remolded, restyled, and made useful again. They beg old neckties, those wide, out-of-style ties with big spiders and cartwheels on them. They rip the stitches out, trim them down, and then make slim-line ties out of these old-style ones which still have good material in them. None of these ideas can be lifted out of textbooks. They must pour out of the heart of a concerned teacher who accepts the youngsters though she may deplore the conditions from which they came.

It is regrettable that we have to embark upon such programs so halfheartedly and with such slim, skeletal budgets as though this were some extra and undesirable aspect of schoolwork. Just as America established her Land Grant colleges for instruction in the mechanic arts, in agriculture, and in home economics, with the results that we are now overproducing food and that we have developed a highly technological society, we must now turn our attention to the problem of the deprived youngsters who are the products of racial discrimination and the slow pace of change. When we faced the exigency of World War II, we produced airplanes at an incredible rate because we were inspired by the will to survive the Nazi nightmare. We need now to convert our efforts with the same dedication to conquer the problems created by the long institution of slavery and a hundred years of discriminatory treatment toward the Negro.

Nothing should be higher on the public policy agenda today than the challenge to harness this innate national impatience and apply the moral and mental energy that this "can do" spirit generates to the misery and the large-scale frustration affecting the Negro masses. Here is an identifiable target on which the focus must be sharpened very early.

Michael Harrington, in *The Other America*,[8] talks about America's "economic underworld." This term he uses to describe the 16,000,000 workers who are not covered by the Minimum Wage Law of 1961—such workers as the domestics, hotel employees, bus boys, dishwashers, and porters in retail stores. These are the city jobs waiting for the Negro farm workers as they disembark from the Trailway Bus. They are jobs uncovered by unions, largely, the back pasture of the job market where the grass is short. Hospital workers in Atlanta, for example, in 1960 could earn $1,000 a year. In Atlanta! Men on dishwashers made 68 cents an hour, maids 55 cents, and kitchen helpers 56 cents. And many so-called liberals still say that the Negro should be doing more for himself to change his status. Do what? Start a bloody workers' revolution? In 1965 the Arkansas legislature defeated a minimum 80 cents-an-hour proposal. What were the Negroes and poor whites earning in that state? Elevator operators 43 cents, maids 64 cents, laundry workers 69 cents, fountain girls 73 cents! Even so, when the Great Society engineers attempt to salvage these humans from the poverty heap, the "right-wingers" yell "creeping social-ism." They never talk of "creeping slavery."

Whatever is done about such jobs, it is still paramount that Negroes train themselves out of this pit of poverty and find their way up the economic ladder. Spelling out the techniques is a task for the educational experts, but embracing the goal should be the task of every concerned American; namely, the opening of new vistas of opportunity for these youngsters so that they may start their movement away from futility, and that the numbers who are descending into this chasm may be reduced. Reading materials, films, and lectures need to be designed by those who can meet these youngsters where they are, who know their jargon, and who can view life through their eyes. Our traditional, anesthetic, piece-meal remedial programs will not be adequate. These programs must be enlarged and become an integral part of the total task of education. Until we adopt a positive attitude in this area, we are going to be beset with rising statistics in crime and delinquency, and the bill will have to be paid in penal costs and in other rehabilitative programs that can at best only half accomplish the desired results.

When we talk of techniques, the ultra-activists call it capitula-tion and a reversion to inertia. Surely the type of activity in which CORE and SNCC have been engaged does have relevance for the total renovation of society. No one likes to admit it, but everyone knows that the sudden burst of concern over Negro problems was as much a desire to get the protest groups away from the down-town streets as it was a quickening of the American conscience and a surge of moral force. Yet, it would be silly to say that marches will bring the young Negro through. Marches and protests performed—and do perform—a function, but it is only a fraction of the total task. Moreover, we may expect one form of protest or another until real progress can be seen. As Bayard Rustin says:

. . . the civil rights movement is evolving from a protest movement into a full-fledged *social movement*—an evolution calling its very name into question. It is now concerned merely with removing the barriers to full *opportunity* but without achieving the fact of *equality*. From sit-ins and freedom rides we have gone into rent strikes, boycotts, community organization, and political action. As a consequence of this natural evolution, the Negro today finds himself stymied by obstacles of far greater magnitude than the legal barriers he was attacking before: automation, urban decay, *de facto* school segregation. . . . These are problems which, while conditioned by Jim Crow, do not vanish upon its demise. They are more deeply rooted in our socio-economic order; they are the result of the total society's failure to meet not only the Negro's needs, but human needs generally.[9]

If America does not find a way to integrate these youngsters into her main corridors of activity and endeavor, they will find other answers. The big surprise is that more Negroes have not already been attracted to movements that are alien to this culture. The Communist party has been a miserable failure among Negroes. In order to account for this, one must understand that the American Negro does not really reject this society totally. He wants to share in it. Marcus Garvey inspired Negroes to parade around Harlem, but they never did board the transports of the Black Star Line and head for the Gold Coast or Port Harcourt. They declined passage in droves! The Negro has no visceral antipathy toward success symbols of the American milieu, but he is hostile toward those who have arbitrarily cut him off short of attaining them, and have shut the doors in his face. If we intend to see the spiral move in the other direction, our practices must involve deliberate procedures that guarantee to the outcast that he is accepted, part of the family, and given the assurance that things are moving in his behalf.

James S. Avery, a young Negro executive of Humble Oil and Refining Company, said this to the 1965 graduating class of Philander Smith College, one of those Methodist, United Negro College Fund affiliated schools which was born in the barren days of the Reconstruction in Arkansas:

It *is* a new day. Opportunities are now open on the broad job front in this country and you can make your own way as long as you bring competence and ability with you. Let us realize that new legal language and new laws of themselves do not assure new opportunities. . . . Every opportunity implies an obligation. Ours is to prepare, to outfit ourselves with the cloak of education and training, just as you graduates have done. It isn't that we have a choice really whether to get it or not . . . we have no choice. Either we develop the skill and utilize our talents to the highest degree, or we end up in a world of lost dreams and unfulfilled opportunity.

What is different about these words in a commencement address? Nothing! The words are so familiar that they could be sung, but what is very different is that the speaker is a Negro in 1965 talking to Negro college students. When that Negro Esso executive speaker finished college, a Negro could only grease cars and change tires at an Esso station, with microscopic exceptions. Had he stood there without saying a word, simply wearing a sign saying "I am an Esso executive," that would have been as eloquent as his well-chosen, though familiar words. He represented a new stage of acceptance.

Those students need every assurance that can be provided that their four years in college were not a long prelude to another dirge of disillusionment. They need a guarantee that the struggle from a cotton farm through organic chemistry, with poverty always closer than a brother and nearer than hands and feet, is worth it.

Acceptance breeds confidence. Not always will this confidence be the outgrowth of some massive social program. More often it will be the result of the individual action of a concerned person. For example, a Negro leader in a southern community visited a 4-H Club program where he delivered an address. He observed that the young student who stood at the lectern introducing him in this small rural school auditorium was extremely talented. When the youngster turned around, the speaker observed further that he had a severe astigmatism commonly called a cross-eyed condition. When the program was over the speaker felt the haunting sense of guilt that something within his own power could be done to correct this visual problem. He asked to talk to the parents and they were suspicious of accepting any such charitable gesture. Moreover, they really believed that the boy's condition was the will of God and should remain as it was. After much persuasion and several visits to this humble rural home, the parents consented to having an operation investigated. The Negro leader telephoned a professor of social ethics at Duke University and asked him to assist him in finding an ophthalmologist willing to invest his skill in this youngster's future. There were several in Durham, North Carolina, and the social ethics professor at Duke eagerly agreed to investigate the possibility of helping this young 4-H Club member.

Eight telephone calls later and after two or three more round trips had been made by the Negro leader to that modest community, the youngster was brought to the hospital for a very simple operation. His eyes were straightened, and he enjoyed the startled response of schoolmates who regarded this as a miracle. This required a very small effort on the part of two adults who were concerned, but if it could become a habit for privileged persons to involve themselves in these one-to-one relationships and invest their experience and insights, the pathway from futility through acceptance to confidence could be discovered by countless young Negroes.

In another instance that illustrates this point, a president of one of the Negro colleges learned that one of his athletes was obliged to leave school. He had played out his eligible seasons of basketball and was finished. His scholarship had run out, and, as in all cases, the coaches had begun to look around for another investment of that scholarship—never in a fifth year for a used-up athlete. After interminable oblique suggestions at the breakfast, lunch, and dinner table, the wife of the president agreed to take this athlete into their home to occupy the guestroom for one semester. He needed a great deal of assistance in small matters, correcting some of those habits that all boys are prone to develop, but which are exaggerated in the lives of those who come from urban Negro ghettos.

This young athlete who had been headed back to the slums without his degree, graduated from college with this small assist. He did his stint in the Army and is now a junior high school teacher in one of the worst slums in the United States. In addition to the result brought about in his life, some other youngsters will benefit from this because he will transmit the concern that was shown for him to the lives of other youngsters far more deprived than he was. Again, the reversal of the spiral can be hastened by multiplying the effective, unscheduled, unprogramed action of individuals with concern above and beyond the massive government and welfare efforts. It may begin with the inspiration of one person who is willing to translate his sentimentality into deeds.

Once their confidence is established and acceptance is guaranteed, these youngsters show that they are willing to participate and to find their place in constructive endeavors. In a project described by Bernstein in that same study, *Youth on the Streets*,[10] he described a meeting at one of the Chicago Youth Development groups. He found the boys folding handbills announcing a movie for which the admission was a can of food to be sent to Negroes in Mississippi. These boys were carried away with enthusiasm because they found themselves doing something constructive with which they could identify and which had deep meaning for them.

In a Youth for Service project in San Francisco, organized by the American Friends Service Committee, youngsters who were known to be hostile and antisocial were given the names of older people living under difficult circumstances. The boys went out in groups, cleaning up and painting the apartments of these elder citizens. Other projects involved building bridges for Indian communities. They were transported and fed by volunteers. The thrill that they got in this experience gave them a new enthusiasm for the whole concept of living a constructive way of life. On one of the projects where they worked in the home of an elderly lady, they were offered pay for their services. They refused it, indicating that this was a volunteer service and that money was not involved.

The Negro people, paradoxically, stand to gain considerably in the long run from the very fact that they have had to develop moral and spiritual muscles to fight their way toward integration. No one should argue that adversity should be invented and imposed for the moral advantage of someone else, but the victims of adversity miss an important point when they fail to translate it into something with meaning. This is difficult for any group to embrace because it represents the net result of many people overcoming natural, human egocentricity and pride.

There must be developed a tradition for pausing in the pursuit of middle-class status symbols and turning in the direction of the forgotten youngsters who are bound in a morass of futility. There are many reasons to feel confident that America will eventually find a way to redeem this element in her population, but individuals who will involve themselves will stand to gain immeasurably from this form of one-to-one involvement. Simeon Booker writes a significant paragraph on this point:

The ghettos, with their atmosphere of failure and defeat, will become the testing ground for the New Negro's versatility. For the first century of freedom, much of our leadership focussed on civil rights iniquities that blotted out hope for a full life. Concentrating on the regaining of a basic dignity, we used integration as a catchword to rouse interest and to put white America on the defensive. In the second century, we must buttress this new dignity with education and training to prepare our people for a much more fruitful life, both in and out of the ghetto. In other words, with a high percentage of Negroes in the ranks of the untrained, unskilled and uneducated, the success of the drive in the years to come will be judged by the gains made in utilizing new opportunities and rehabilitating the masses. How fast the ghettos disappear will be determined more by how soon Negroes can be trained and qualified to take their place in society.[11]

The involvement of the Federal Anti-Poverty Program is most encouraging. There are inevitable problems in some of these programs, especially the community action, multipurpose attack on joblessness, dropouts, unwed mothers, consumer education needs, literacy training, and legal counseling. There will be problems especially in the Job Corps and Neighborhood Youth Corps. The youngsters who are recruited for this program are not college freshmen, and they would not be in this program if their communities had succeeded in opening up to them constructive channels toward fulfillment. There will be deviate conduct. There will be acts of violence. They will not be able to jump completely clear of their previous affiliations, attitudes, and values into a new world of meaning and purpose in nine months. If the American public is really concerned, it will be sympathetic, understanding, and will not expect this program to begin as a Twentieth Century wonder any more than open heart surgery or the expeditions to the moon were immediate first-stage successes. Nevertheless, as these programs expand, we expect to see less and less indifference toward poverty, a deeper concern for what happens to poor people, more restlessness among the poor, and no place at all for those communities that attempt to ignore the fact that the poor are among them. In very practical terms, just as many Americans found assistance through the NYA program in the thirties and forties to complete college education, many will find in the college work and scholarship programs of the Economic Opportunity Act the only real assistance enabling them to enter or to remain in college. The results of this will be shown not only in terms of renewed lives, but in the economic dividends that come when thousands of youngsters return to their home towns with capacity for high-level employment, rather than remain around unemployed, underemployed, on welfare, and in penal and rehabilitation programs. This is a terrific bargain! This is indeed a direct assault on that kind of poverty that has passed down from one generation to another in the same family. A federal loan or scholarship can make a clean break in the legacy of poverty. This is surely the type of bold public effort that it will require to move the spiral into reverse.

Of course, it is rather late to begin at the college level. Effective endeavor must begin at the very earliest practical date, the first level at which the child is person enough to begin responding to teaching and to his surroundings. The Headstart program is very effective. It says to a youngster that he will not be penalized because of the accident of his birth in a deprived neighborhood. It says that his government is concerned enough about reversing the spiral that threatens to move his life toward futility, that it is willing to invest significantly in his earliest, formative years, correcting dental problems, visual problems, nutrition deficiencies, and cultural isolation. His beginning in school, hopefully, will be more nearly at dead level with his more fortunate contemporaries. As his life begins on this plane, he will not have to suffer from an ever-widening gap between his own performance and that of his privileged classmates. Senior classes in high school all across the country will represent a far greater percentage of those who entered the first grade largely because of the Headstart program. It is simply a question of preparing a child for basic learning experiences to offset the failure of his poverty-ridden early childhood.

As we conclude this discussion of the spiral that moves to futility, let us be sure that the main point is clear: America's concern for deprived Negro youths should not be motivated by a desire to see markets improved, tax money saved, or a good image projected before the dark-skinned people of the world. It should be because our nation was conceived in the conviction that every individual has inherent worth. However disastrous may be the results of the slave system and the one hundred years of discriminatory treatment that followed, we should not stand helpless before the immensity of the problem. We should apply to this the same ingenuity and courage that we have engaged in facing every other crisis in our history. It is clear to us that the Negro will not be content to be second-class, relegated to a position of interminable inferiority. The task is to devise means by which these lives can be salvaged and made an integral part of the great American experience.

We have talked about those Negro youths who, on their own, asserted their desire to be emancipated from an inferior status. They will make it. They will demonstrate, protest, sue, and fight their way to freedom. They have an appreciation of their own sense of worth, and nothing will stop them. The more obstacles society places in their path, the stronger they will become in overcoming them. But the helpless ones who began life with more severe disadvantages need another approach. Charity is not a good word in America, but this is exactly what they need: charity in its best sense. Love which is not selfish, seeking its own gratification; love which is not reciprocal, trading favors; but love which is redemptive, which cares for the object loved and which is compelled by the knowledge that the lover has been loved himself with a quality of love that reaches its finest when it is transmitted to someone else. It is a love that pursues its object in spite of its worthlessness and that takes no account of its capacity to reciprocate. We find our own fulfillment in the lives of others. This cannot remain an academic concept for us, but a living, vital reality in our private concerns and in our public programs.

4

Overcoming the Deficits in Education

THE topic of Education and the Negro is explosive. The main hope is that the generation rising through the educational processes today will bring to its adult years a greater competence to deal with the problem of erasing the color bar in America. This will require immediate resolution to integrate all schools and to improve schools where Negroes are still compelled to remain segregated because of inertia in the Negro community and resistance in the white.

The civil rights movement rightfully sees as its target a system of denial and discrimination that must be destroyed before the Negro people can change their status and find freedom. As this target is pursued, the sad fact remains that life goes on and millions of Negroes have to do something at 8:15 tomorrow morning within the process of their own lives and with whatever personal equipment they happen to have.

The Existent Deficit

Greater emphasis, however, needs to be placed upon the deficit which now exists and upon the necessity of the young Negro to take a hard look at the price that America will demand in an impersonal way from anyone who presents himself for inclusion with gaps and deficiencies in his education.

The incendiary nature of the problem is far more than the question of using a bus to transport pupils or pairing schools to effect integration. It has to do with America's deep intent. The inferior status of the Negro has been guaranteed by inferior education. It follows that equal educational opportunity would undo this whole sinister scheme and bring the nation to the greatest moment of truth that it has ever had to face in the area of race. It is one thing to have to make room for a relatively few well-prepared Negroes, but equal education will destroy the correlation of the Negro people with crime, with disease, with delinquency, and with "cultural lag." It will level Negro children off with the test scores and the other indices of readiness that characterize other children. It will play havoc with the spurious anthropology that has haunted us for so long. It will mean dealing with Negroes at dead eye level, not as objects of mercy or as candidates for special effort. It may take two school generations, but if equal educational opportunity is offered, it will surely come.

Consequently, the topic is explosive. The young Negro, bold and eager to go all the way, has lit the fuse. Here we stand with our eyes closed, our lips puckered, our toes turned in to each other, our knees bent and shaking, with fingers plugging each ear to muffle the sound. The debate resounds throughout the land. We have to decide if we really want equality and a showdown with racist theories. If we do, we have to get busy at equal education.

For our purpose, however, we need to carve out that segment of the discussion which has greatest relevance for the young Negro as he charges forth toward equality by the time his children are ready to be the adult generation, let us say, 1980. Many generalizations will have to be allowed and much rebuttal will have to be left unheard. In fact, the 1980 target is based on a surmise that the young Negro wants to see in the lives of his children what is just a promise in his own lifetime.

We should raise five questions, at least: (1) Is the young Negro aware of his educational deficit? (2) How long has this deficit been accumulating? (3) What counterefforts have abated it? (4) How can it be checked, now? (5) What posture should the young

Negro assume while remedies are getting started and before their cures reach his present advanced condition?

The Cumulative Effect of Poor Education

As the young Negro leaps forward in pursuit of equality he is discovering to his frustration that the deficits in his education are a serious weight. For example, when the best-intentioned graduate school deans examine his record, transcript, and recommendations and compare these credentials with such indices as Scholastic Aptitude Test Scores and Graduate Record Examination Scores, the two sets of credentials too frequently do not match. The admissions officer then faces the dilemma: Should he admit this Negro with inferior preparation and lower the standard of his institution? Or, should he deny him an opportunity and thereby prevent him from getting whatever advanced education he might receive, even if he had to drag along at a lower-than-average level of performance? Most often, the latter course is followed, and it is not unusual for the Negro graduate student to make an honest assessment of his problem and put in the extra time required in the library and laboratory to overcome his deficit. No matter whatever else may be done in his behalf, the deficit becomes a very personal problem and it must be offset by the most resolute determination of the individual.

Whatever he does, wherever he turns and finds himself measured against these criteria that are generally used to gauge intellectual competence in American life, he is reminded of his deficiencies. His vivid recollection of his segregated, inferior school, his poorly trained teachers, his crowded classrooms, and perhaps a late, personal decision that he wanted to achieve serve to mitigate the situation and lessen the frustration. He learns to face his condition like a man recently gone blind. People keep talking of things he vaguely remembers but which were not thoroughly etched on his mind. He never thought such etching would make the difference between survival and a clumsy stumbling through life.

Unfortunately, many of them are naïve about this and present their degrees and diplomas with deficient training insisting that they are qualified on the basis of their records. The fact is that the quality of education offered to them was limited by their lack of earlier adequate preparation, more than likely by the lack of preparation on the part of their teachers also, the cultural atmosphere in which they spent their leisure time, and the indifference of those in authority toward the problem of improving their educational opportunities. All this has resulted in a critical distance between the average Negro and his white counterpart by almost any educational standard.

As young Negroes strike out from their rural origins in the South, their urban, segregated communities of the North, and the large southern towns that have completely dual arrangements with all the trimmings, they gravitate invariably toward the larger commercial centers where jobs are available and where the political climate is ostensibly more favorable toward them. This movement, in competition with better-trained whites, especially of the North, exposes their educational deficit in gigantic proportions.

A test is required for almost everything in American life. Some of these tests are designed as a device to control the flow of applications and to screen out Negroes, Puerto Ricans, and those of Asian origin. That they have been used effectively is not any longer debatable. But this is not always the motive for requiring tests. The country is test-oriented. It derives in part from reforms in the Civil Service system and the whole effort to get the best-qualified persons into the right jobs without preferentialism. When this principle is applied to the Negro applicant, he simply suffers, because he has been robbed educationally all his life. As his mobility increases, these reports about him are spread into every crevice of the job market.

One may summarize this point with the generalization that by the age of twelve the average Negro is more than two full years behind the average white in terms of measurable educational achievements. By the time he is a high school graduate at eighteen, the Negro has fallen three years behind. If he goes to an inferior college, upon graduation his degree should be equated with a high school diploma from one of the better high schools in a well-financed and well-staffed school district.

Others who have worked with this problem state it differently, widening or closing the gap, but always with little variation. Whitney Young says: ". . . [the] Negro youngster receives three and one-half years less schooling than the average white child. When one considers that the bulk of elementary training for the Negro child is received in inferior, segregated, slum schools—

North and South—then the real difference is more accurately five years."[1]

In order to appreciate fully how the cumulative effect of poor education over a long period influences current problems, let us take a look at a case history. Negroes from Mississippi, for example, migrate to Chicago, following the main railroad lines. Consider, therefore, that the children in the public schools of Chicago today were reared in homes under the influences of parents who spent their youth in Mississippi. In Mississippi they grew up on tenant farms and in the colored sections of small towns amid the cultural limitations of their parents, the grandparents of today's Chicago school children. Let us say that the grandparents were young school children in the early 1900's. Then remember what Governor James K. Vardaman said in 1907. In his campaign for re-election he boasted that he had kept an election pledge to keep public school funds from flowing into black counties. He boasted that this point dominated his inaugural address. He made this a prime campaign issue, demonstrating his fitness for re-election. In other words, in 1907 the principal plank in the platform of the Governor of Mississippi was his guarantee to keep Negroes ignorant. And he boasted of the success that he had had in this endeavor during his first term. Governor Vardaman was a man brazen enough to say such things publicly, but the same attitude prevailed in many other sections of the South. It is probably true that the young Negro has very little conception of these depths of the roots of this problem in his background and, hence, very little understanding of the efforts that will have to be made in order to overcome a deficit that has been so long accumulating.

North Carolina has always been a more liberal southern state, but in 1883 the North Carolina Legislature passed a law which provided that Negro schools had to be supported by Negro tax income only and that white tax income would be spent only on white schools. The intent was obvious. It was a deliberate scheme to cripple the black folk educationally so that they would have to go hobbling through American life intellectually crippled. It is interesting that when this was done, decent white people sought to rationalize the effort and make it sound morally defensible. Frenise Logan, in *The Negro in North Carolina, 1876–1894*,[2] summarized one of the prevailing weak arguments. It went somewhat like this: Since the white people are not willing to invest more tax money in education, their attitude could be changed if they knew that their tax money went for white schools only. This would mean the improvement of white schools, and since Negroes have a tendency to imitate, in the long run, this would be beneficial because the Negroes would then be imitating better schools.

Even during those dark days after the Tilden-Hayes election, when the Negroes saw their educational gains slipping through their fingers rapidly, they maintained their sanity by ridiculing this hate-inspired movement. In the midst of the debate on this 1883 school bill in North Carolina, which required the Negroes to pay for their own schools out of their own taxes, one of the three Negro members of the North Carolina Senate, Robert R. Gray, offered an amendment. He moved that the bill should go all the way and that where a white man had children of both races, white children by his legal white wife and fair-skinned, straight-haired, gray-eyed children by his Negro mistress, his tax money should be divided to go for the education of all his children, his white children as well as his mulatto offspring. The Senate rejected this amendment.

Returning to the study of the Negro in North Carolina by Frenise Logan, his work reveals that the deficits in Negro education were more deliberately planned than we commonly are led to believe, for there is considerable evidence for the fact that the Negroes made a fast start in pursuit of learning. They were eager for training during the earliest days after the Emancipation. There is much to be learned from a close reading of Reconstruction literature on this topic. For example, some of the white leadership feared that the future of the whites was endangered by the rapid pace of the education of the Negroes. In 1888, a speech made by F. T. Venable before the North Carolina Historical Society made the point that Anglo-Saxon supremacy in North Carolina could not be maintained unless the whites did something to balance the Negroes' aggressiveness in striving for education.[3] Other newspaper reports and editorials exclaimed that the Negroes were improving faster than the whites and deplored the fact that the whites were insufficiently interested in getting their children into schools.

As early as 1888 there were more than 1000 members of the North Carolina State Teachers Association, an organization of Negro educators, founded in 1880! The records show that they were doing some things then that they do not do today, such as establishing reading circles to introduce to the Negro teachers the best publications in pedagogy. As early as 1876, a mere thirteen years after the Emancipation, there were 817 Negro teachers as compared with 2,077 white teachers. This is an incredibly fast beginning for people emerging out of slavery.

Counterefforts to Abate the Deficit

Among the southern states, North Carolina has always been a leader in education for Negroes. The disparity in per-pupil expenditure in 1880 was not nearly so great as one would imagine: $1.47 spent on each white pupil and $1.38 spent on each Negro pupil. Fourteen years later, it was $1.93 spent per white pupil and $1.72 per Negro. This difference may seem unimportant, but this accounts for the progress that North Carolina Negroes have been able to make in successive years as compared with Negroes from states in the deeper South where they were not given as much encouragement in getting an education. The results in North Carolina were commensurately significant. Illiteracy among Negroes declined from 77 per cent in 1880 to 47 per cent in 1900.

In higher education in North Carolina the churches gave early and significant leadership. As early as 1763 the Anglican Church had established institutions for Indians and Negroes. This movement grew slowly, reaching its crescendo in the first ten years following the Emancipation. The Presbyterians established Scotia Seminary, now Barber-Scotia College at Concord, for Negro women in 1870, and in 1884 there was an enrollment of 242 students. By 1884 this college had to close admissions in early summer because of the swelling number of applicants. The African Methodist Episcopal Zion Church took great pride in the establishment of Livingstone College at Salisbury. Many prominent Negroes today, who are active leaders on the American scene, secured their undergraduate training from institutions established in these early days following the Emancipation. Edward R. Dudley, for example, who was recently borough president of Manhattan and earlier ambassador to Liberia, is an alumnus of Johnson C. Smith University, another Presbyterian college established in the early days following Reconstruction. Ambassador James Nabrit, United States delegate to the United Nations Security Council, is a Morehouse College graduate. So is Dr. Martin Luther King. Commander Samuel Gravely, highest ranking Negro in the Navy and captain of a destroyer based in San Diego, is from Richmond's Virginia Union University. Judge J. Earl Dearing, City Prosecutor, Police Court, Louisville, Kentucky, is likewise an alumnus of Virginia Union University. Dr. Matthew Carter, the Deputy Mayor of Montclair, New Jersey, is from that school also. James Farmer is from Wylie College, a Methodist school in Marshall, Texas; and the Solicitor-General of the United States, Thurgood Marshall, is from the oldest Negro college, Lincoln University in Pennsylvania.

Shaw University, founded as a co-operative endeavor with support from Baptists of North Carolina and the American Baptist Home Mission Society, had a very ambitious beginning. With appliances and equipment imported from France, a medical college was founded. Some of these early graduates are still practicing medicine all over the United States. This story could be repeated regarding many, many sections of the South. In 1876 the Southern Presbyterians founded Stillman College at Tuscaloosa, Alabama. Morehouse College in Atlanta, whose graduates have made such strong contributions to the cause of Negro freedom as well as in America's national life in general, was the product of the American Baptist Home Mission Society and other co-operating Baptists in Georgia. When Henry L. Morehouse, the man for whom that school is named, was seeking to raise funds to strengthen the growth of this college during its formative years, he was heard to speak vehemently in behalf of the education of Negroes. He said, "I believe in the very humanity of the black man, capable of culture, capable of high attainment with sufficient time and under proper circumstances, not a being foreordained to be a hewer of wood and a drawer of water for the white race, predestined to irrevocable inferiority, but a being whose mind and soul can expand indefinitely, to comprehend the great things of God and to take a place of usefulness and honor in the world's activities." It may be that he dreamed of having alumni of that college serving as jurists, researchers, government executives, college presidents, and emissaries of America's government to the far-flung corners of the world. The record of Morehouse men is an enviable one indeed.

Virginia Union University began in a jail in Richmond. When other properties were unavailable, the founders of that institution purchased a jail which had been used for incorrigible slaves.

Today, among its alumni are men like attorney Wesley Williams, president of the Washington, D.C., school board, a half-dozen college presidents, the late Eugene Kinkle Jones who was the early long-term executive director of the National Urban League, the late distinguished father of Congressman Adam Clayton Powell, and Judge Homer Brown of Pittsburgh.

It is instructive to look at the record of some of the very productive Negro families, and to trace their intellectual genealogy: the Nabrits—Samuel, who is president of Texas Southern University, and James, on leave at UNESCO from the presidency of Howard University; the Clements of Kentucky; the Danielses of Virginia; the Davises of Hampton; the Hendersons of Newport News. These are families in which several brothers and sisters in each hold three degrees, several doctorates among them. They were trained and inspired by teachers who finished these schools founded in travail during Reconstruction. One wonders what on earth would have been the plight of Negro people today without the early founding of colleges for Negroes and the early dawning of hope in the breasts of Negro people that caused them to want to be educated. Practically every prominent Negro today can trace the origin of his intellectual development to some black pilgrim who trod the dusty roads of a rural Negro community to enroll in one of these small colleges established on the faith hypothesis that these dark-skinned people were not some subhuman specie but were capable of responding to the process of education. Had these people waited until the hearts of the whites were changed and admission to established white institutions was made available to them, the educational deficit that we now deplore would be incalculably greater.

To Scrap or Not to Scrap Negro Colleges?

This brings us to a very important and controversial point. Should the Negroes scrap these institutions now because they cannot meet comparative standards with the finest of Ivy League colleges? Should their graduates be ashamed to wear the alumni label from these schools because they were founded for Negroes and because they are still identified as Negro colleges? What does America stand to gain or to lose by continuing this phenomenon of Negro colleges? The question is far more than an academic one because it has to do with how much actual support is given these institutions and what attitude should be taken toward their graduates, today, tomorrow, and next week.

We have seen the deliberate effort to impede the educational progress of Negroes in the early days and the persistence of Negroes in quest of training. Do the colleges founded for Negroes, which accomplished so much, constitute an anachronism today? Do they have any unique, viable role to play in overcoming the educational deficit? The private Negro colleges are producing better than 10,000 graduates a year who are deployed into the communities of the South and the North giving leadership in the Negro community and opening doors that have been previously closed to Negroes.

Those who are closest to the situation have the least doubt about the answer to the question regarding their usefulness, for they know that among these thirty-odd private colleges there are nearly fifty thousand students. In addition, there are over 125,000 Negro students enrolled in the more than thirty state colleges established for Negroes in the seventeen southern states. Of course, in order to justify continuing these schools, keeping them strong, and developing them in size and in influence, the moral corollary must be that any Negro student who wishes to matriculate at a private or public institution that was previously all white should be permitted and encouraged to do so. Moreover, since the Negro colleges were created for persons who were not only racially distinguishable but who also bore all the marks of economic and social disadvantage, these colleges will surely become an integral part of American higher education, attracting white students also who for financial, social, or intellectual reasons cannot, or do not choose to go to other institutions. Whitney Young reinforces this point:

Many of these schools today represent the major, if not the only, centers of cultural influence existing in some communities for white as well as Negro citizens. This role will expand. In addition, the number of white students and foreign students in these institutions will increase beyond their present enrollment and interracial faculties will become more commonplace. There is a healthy trend toward the development of more cooperative faculty exchange programs with other leading universities as a spur to greater academic growth. It is, therefore, unreasonable to suppose that these institutions will disappear at a time when the nation is faced with a serious shortage of classroom facilities.[4]

It is ironical to hear arguments in favor of their closing which present as evidence factors that would also close scores of white colleges of the same size and some with even more meager resources. If one argued to close Hampton Institute or Tuskegee Institute because it was an allegedly weak college, it would follow that every college with less than twenty million dollars of endowment, with fewer than fifty Ph.D.s on the faculty, and with campuses less attractive and developed than Hampton and Tuskegee should be closed also. There would not be many small colleges left in America if this logic were followed. Then why should Hampton Institute be closed? Should it be penalized because it was founded to meet the needs of a peculiar people at a peculiar moment, especially since those same needs still are with us? Why can it not undergo its own metamorphosis and become just another college, and lose no time in making the adjustment from a strictly Negro college to one with an integrated student body? The time that this change requires may be a good measure of the time that America will require to readjust to the other demands of the rising young Negro.

An artificial conclusion or an assumption that the closing of the colleges signals a new day that has not really come could actually postpone the coming of that day by arbitrarily limiting the number of Negroes who can find a college education. And, when we say that the average Negro college alumnus holds a diploma that is four years weaker than the average from other institutions, many of these schools do have equipment that is *above the average* and many "white" colleges are also four years *behind the average.*

Many of these schools boast now that they are integrated, but in fact they are not. The number of white students enrolled is infinitesimal. The reasons why some of the whites are enrolled go further to make the claim ludicrous. This token and often sensational integration should not have to be an argument for their existence. They are doing an educational job for youngsters who live close to them and who have some cultural affinity with the institution and its heritage. There needs to be no other reason, no more reason than a blonde, blue-eyed Lutheran would have to give for wanting to go to St. Olaf in Minnesota or to a smaller Lutheran college like Newberry in South Carolina.

This issue is worth pursuing further, for if anything in Negro life represents the cohesiveness, the continuity, the real self-consciousness of Negro life in America, it is the Negro college. These schools produced the Negro "greats" and created that early self-image of the Negro that saw him through the disheartening setbacks of the eighties and the nineties, the cruelties of the lynch parties of the twenties and the insults and indignities of the rigid white supremacy of the thirties, and brought him to the forties standing tall and ready to embrace his legal campaign to destroy segregation.

There is so much impulsiveness in the discussions about education that the issue of the Negro colleges is likely to be glossed over as a small matter that history will take care of. But the fact still is that the bulk of adult Negroes holding college degrees came from these institutions. Negro enrollment in northern colleges and universities is a pitiable trickle, and the enrollment of the 125,000 in the colleges of the South turns out to be the only big hope. The hope is even bigger because they are in the South where the problems are gravest, the black population the highest, and resistance to the extension of opportunity the most intransigent.

This is not a light matter, given the elements that make for change. These elements must include the increase in the numbers of better-qualified Negroes with an impatience with denial and inequality and a readiness on the part of America to open doors to them. The moment is now; and, if the doors are opening, they are largely opening to Negroes in terms of those 125,000 and more in the state colleges strung across the South.

If the movement toward integration is going to mean the unmitigated denial of all that Negroes have created institutionally, leaving nothing reminiscent of a separate society, the colleges will have to go. That is where we come out with such logic. If the process will allow a transformation of these institutions, lodges, churches, barber shops, mortuaries and night clubs, with integration moving from the public facilities and institutions to the smaller circle of private institutions, then these colleges will be the most reliable laboratory for testing how fast this metamorphosis will take place. They will aid the process by doing their job so well that they will work themselves out of existence as Negro colleges.

The major foundations of the country are beginning to respond to the needs of these institutions in a wide variety of efforts. This interest has grown and kept pace with the total national interest in Negroes since 1960. The Rockefeller family has long shown an interest in these schools, but it is correct to say that the foundations generally have only recently made relatively sizable grants to these schools in recognition of the Negroes' bid for total emancipation.

Significant help has been forthcoming from the Carnegie, Ford, Rockefeller, Danforth, Field, Sloane, Johnson, Esso, Woodrow Wilson, Taconic, and smaller foundations. The grants have taken the form of support for remedial reading and mathematics instruction, fine arts, summer institutes for teachers in selected disciplines in Negro colleges, and faculty exchanges between Negro colleges and "white" universities. These "big brother" relationships exist between the following institutions:

Brown University and Tougaloo College in Mississippi
Hampton Institute and Cornell University
University of Wisconsin and both A&T College of North Carolina,
    North Carolina College at Durham, and Texas Southern University
Tuskegee Institute in Alabama and University of Michigan
Stillman College of Alabama and Indiana University
University of Tennessee and Knoxville College
Florida A&M University and Florida State University
Winston-Salem State College and Southern Illinois University

There are other tangential relationships involving student exchanges and special programs and consortia on regional bases, especially in university centers in Virginia and in Piedmont, N.C.

The significance of these efforts is that relatively large sums of private resources are at last reaching the bedrock of the Negro problem, the production of young people who will be academically prepared to give sustained and sizable leadership in education and—hence—on every front. For years these Negro colleges were the stepchildren of the collegiate family, and to their problems of money were added problems of isolation and embarrassment.

Perhaps the greatest benefit of the foundations' endeavor is the impetus that this effort and the influence of the ideas projected have had upon the United States Office of Education. Government representatives have sat in on many of the brainstorming sessions, and it is no surprise that the 1965 Higher Education Act raises a federal umbrella over practically every facet of the challenge that these colleges face in doing much better work with Negro youth who are still looking to them for educational opportunity. The hope is that these schools will soon level off as good colleges for the nation without a racial tag.

The side effects of these intercampus exchanges will be extensive in helping to achieve an understanding of Negroes far beyond their intent. When the English professor from Brown shall have finished telling Tougaloo students about dangling participles, and the Indiana historians shall have told Stillman youngsters from Alabama hills all about Machiavelli, and Wisconsin researchers shall have shared their techniques and processes with Texas and North Carolina students, these visitors will go back to Providence, Bloomington, and Milwaukee with far more than the intrinsic satisfaction of having done something worthwhile in life. They will take back an authentic understanding of what alienation and separation can do to a young mind, how crippling inferior grade-school training can be, and what a miracle it is that any sizable number of Negroes survive without incurable defeatism. In their circles back home, where middle-class whites are curious about the amorphous nature of the "Negro" problem, these returning professors—among other things—will be important sources of enlightenment and understanding. We have not had this academic "Peace Corps" before—at least in recent times and on such a scale—and we should expect to gain just as much from this as we do from our efforts in the international Peace Corps.

The logic is sound behind the strengthening of the colleges and the demand to increase, rather than decrease, the number of colleges available to American youth; there is strategic importance in having colleges in major southern cities where social transitions are merely beginning; it is a gain that Negro-managed institutions are meeting national competition on a continuing basis with biracial faculties and student enrollments; and there is a psychological plus in the total social equation of the 175,000 students in these colleges making their way through government and business, education and technology with degrees from colleges that began as the illegitimate offspring of American higher education. Yet, there is still the strong, prevailing suspicion that such logic is the minion of a scheme to procrastinate on the whole issue of including Negroes now in the total fabric of American education.

To be sure, there are racists who would sponsor the perpetuation of these colleges for the worst possible of all reasons—to shackle Negro youth indefinitely with weak, superficial education and fraudulent degrees. A serious discussion of the issue should not bog down in the mire of debate on this point. It should not be dignified by response, for it would be criminal if the colleges were kept going for this reason. Yet, this fear has been constantly acknowledged and has become part of the conundrum that has deferred positive, aggressive action to strengthen these schools.

The situation calls for a more profound understanding of the plight of Negro youth today and for the best leverage for lifting them out of the chasm of disadvantage. The perfect option of absolute integration is not a live one. The perfect antecedents for this option do not exist. The facts are painfully clear: Negro youth do have inferior high school preparation; there is reluctance on the part of colleges everywhere to admit them and give the extra help that would compensate for their deficits; improvement in secondary education is in process but far from adequate; there will be 175,000 Negro students in these colleges in 1966; they should not be denied training at their level of achievement; there are many "white" colleges functioning without apology at the same level of educational thrust as many of the "Negro" schools; graduates of these colleges already comprise the critical mass of Negro leadership all over the country; the loss of the annual production of 20,000 Negro youth, even with mediocre degrees, would effect a dramatic slowdown in Negro progress and create a leadership gap in many communities in the South for the next twenty years that would leave the Negroes extremely vulnerable to a "Birchite" backlash from the right and a seductive, "anti-establishment" tryst from the left.

Already, evidence abounds to prove that an emphasis upon education for full black emancipation is more than middle-class escapism. Whatever other aspects of "the movement" that may prove effective will have to presuppose a grass-roots base of responsible, educated leadership. There must be a rapid swell in the numbers of Negroes ready to negotiate with the power structure for immediate changes in school desegregation, revised housing patterns, new job openings and a greater share in the policymaking for anti-poverty and urban renewal programs. Moreover, the tremendous gains that reapportionment can lead toward will require a diaspora of Negroes providing a network of educated political interpreters covering every urban complex.

At whatever point in time a given community is ready to face its moment of truth on the matter of racial justice, there must be, not standing waiting, but deeply involved and clearly identified, a vanguard of disciplined, trained and perceptive Negroes, angry enough to be indignant at deceptive bribes and invitations to create a new "Uncle Tomism," but smart enough to convert this anger into programs for real change the moment reapproachment begins to appear.

Many programs will require the insights of the black poor who may not hold degrees. A college degree is not essential for a clear grasp of the racial dimensions of poverty. Yet, trained Negroes allied with the poor in sincere, cooperative endeavor comprise an excellent combination for responsible action.

Improving Still-Segregated Southern Public Schools

This brings us to another consideration regarding the public schools of the South. Everyone knows that as long as they remain segregated they will reflect the continuing dual patterns of the entire social structure of the South. They will help to make this pattern even more indelible by educating the young to accept this duality as inevitable. Everyone knows also that by the time a school faculty adjusts itself to the level of expectation which the Negro pupils bring from the ghettos, that school automatically will have taken on a weaker intellectual thrust than the schools for the more privileged whites. But does it follow, therefore, that the Negro schools that presently exist should not be improved? Does it follow that such schools—thousands!—should not be strengthened? How many youngsters can we afford to sacrifice by denying improvements in the Negro schools while working for the end of the racially separate system?

Today, years after the 1954 decision, we still find the vast majority of Negroes in Negro schools, following residential patterns. Even yet, there is more noise and talk than there is actual programing for integration. Many schools in the South are enrolling just enough Negroes to slide a quarter of an inch inside the law to qualify for federal grants. They call it integration, but only where the Negro population is very small do we really see integration. When there are enough Negro children to fill up a school, they have their own! Few exceptions are seen.

There is an atmosphere in the urban South that gives encouragement to those who want to see permanent segregation in schools. There are hundreds of Negro teachers, working in their home towns, enjoying better salaries than most people, and constituting a major segment of a secure, home-owning middle class. With their husbands' jobs, these families have a steady income of $15,000 to $18,000 a year; and they are therefore the very backbone of the Negro people in the South. They have beautiful homes, lawns, and terraces. They have a delightful and casual social life and enjoy the respect of the entire town.

This did not come about yesterday. This Negro "schoolteacher" class is a 90-year development, and it is solid. There is no enthusiasm at all among this group to dissolve the complex of Negro institutional life. They will see to it that it stays intact. It is a silent consent that requires no debate. When the discussion gets to the deciding point they remember that the children have to be picked up at the newly integrated theater, or the son is flying in from prep school and must be met momentarily at the airport.

There is this class, this society, that thrives on "Negro" schools. There is no other employment open in such volume and at such pay. It will not commit suicide.

The paradox is that many of these same people send their own children to "white" schools, many were the first to enter "white" graduate schools and they have a cogent, logical position that segregation must go. They are a type of Negroes able to enjoy newly integrated hotels, theaters and restaurants.

When we focus on the Negro school and say that it must go before society is ready to budge on housing, on recreation, or on jobs that this class can get, they just stand pat and give only a nodding consent. For them the issue is not so simple as that, and any defense that they vocalize is likely to be put to music by both the civil rights leadership and the segregationist politicians.

In their private moments, especially after a tongue-loosing bourbon and ginger ale, they say that civil rights leadership is a profession that thrives not only on the vulnerability of white guilt, but likewise on the vulnerability of the only thing Negroes have: that solid, church-going, degree-getting, money-saving, big-consuming, dues-paying, home-buying Negro middle class that interlaces the South, that keeps good-looking, well-dressed women pushing Buicks and Mercurys up and down the wide and endless new federal highways, rushing to weddings, bridges, coffeeklatsches, farewell parties, formal dances, and committee meetings. They fought to get out of white kitchens and laundries. The threat of going back, or of having to move to the tombs of Newark, Pittsburgh, or Brooklyn, is not frightening because they will not allow it to sink into consciousness.

Meanwhile, segregation goes on. An approach to the issue that deals honestly with the children and that recognizes the inertia among whites and the caution among the Negro "schoolteacher" class must be found and pursued. Indeed, it seems to have emerged already. The strategy that seems to be coming at us out of the walls is this:

A. Challenge school segregation everywhere and keep the pressure on for an inclusive system. This will keep a stream of Negroes moving into previously all-white schools at every level.

B. Keep the job market expanding to relieve the fears that teaching in a Negro school is the only decent job an educated Negro can get.

C. Make no peace with segregated housing; encourage a growing campaign to have Negro families on display in every section of every city.

D. While pursuing these goals see to it that the Negro pupils who are still in Negro schools get the best equipment, best instruction, and best faculty personnel available.

We simply cannot turn our backs on the children in the Negro schools, illegal and immoral as such schools are, while the issue of "bussing," "pairing," new schools, redistricting, and so on, are being resolved. The pupils are there now. Dr. Kenneth B. Clark, the real expert in this area, whose testimony was so vital to the 1954 decision, says this on the point at hand:

A number of individuals prominent in the civil rights movement claim, however, that a demand for excellence in ghetto schools is really camouflage for acquiescence in segregation. On the contrary it is, given the intransigence of the white community and the impossibility of immediate integration, a decision to save as many Negro children as possible now. The struggle of the civil rights groups for a better life for these children is made more difficult, if not impossible, if the methods of the struggle become dominated by inflexible emotional postures. . . . These children, Negro or white, must not be sacrificed on the altars of ideological and semantic rigidities.[5]

It is possible that a large number of young Negroes will suffer because the moral grounds for segregated schools are so untenable, and the civil rights leadership so vigilant, that professional educators cannot devote adequate attention to the job of improving the school where the Negroes are actually currently enrolled. There should be a better answer to this because the generation now in school is perhaps the most crucial one that Negroes will ever see. They must be ready to walk into the new areas of opportunity now being opened. As Simeon Booker has said: "We must not squander the tomorrow of three million two hundred fifty thousand-odd Negro school children in the South, who need better facilities, better libraries and incentives."[6]

It is not likely that Alabama and Mississippi, and most of Virginia, South Carolina, and Louisiana, will arrange for the complete integration of their schools very soon. These states will do what is required, and there will be footwork and circumvention practiced for quite some time to forestall complete integration.

It behooves every Negro principal and every Negro teacher to do everything he can with every minute at his disposal to help every child to reach his fullest potential. He should get every facility, every book, and every microscope he can. He should improve the school in every detail and after school join those forces that work to erase the housing lines, and that press for the integration of the entirety of society. We have as much reason to count on their integrity in this as we do in counting on the integrity of the managers of education to integrate at an early date.

The South has 12,000,000 Negroes. Bitterness runs high. Racial lines are not receding fast. They will move faster as more of the millions of whites and Negroes improve economically and throw back the veils of ignorance and fear from their eyes. We know that more is to be gained by full integration and we must settle for nothing less. Anything less is to grant credence to the arguments for segregation. But the Negro must be smart enough to count the heads in Negro schools today and press for the best for them now, where they are, thus hastening the day when they, too, will be measuring arms with their white contemporaries and converting one good school after another into an integrated one.

As we turn from the picture in the South, we find a far more complicated situation in the North. The schools in the North are segregated in the big cities. Some integration is promoted, but faithlessly. Negroes live as separate and as apart in the North as they do elsewhere; but there is a little more tolerance, more give in the seams and it should be stretched now.

The Segregated Public Schools of the North

As a first step, the North should forsake the notion of creating a Negro enclave with a brand-new school in the center. After all, the South stumbled into its pattern by virtue of the slave system folding up with 4,000,000 Negroes still on the premises. There is far more guilt on the part of the North if it deliberately seeks to create a situation to match the South.

New schools should be built on the lines between communities to promote integration; good schools near each other should split up their grades and divide their pupils to cause immediate integration. Where it is feasible, pupils should be transported out of the ghetto to better unfilled schools, and Negroes should press for open enrollment where the structures impede automatic integrated enrollment. These measures will correct the evil in the present exigency as far as it can be corrected until we get rid of the discriminatory housing and liquidate every ghetto.

But the North faces another enormous problem: the migration of hordes of Negroes from the rural South, transplanting the neglect that they have suffered there. In community after community on Long Island, for example, there are very highly educated whites occupying a delightful suburb and demanding the best things for their children in terms of education and culture. There is also a colony of Negro domestics and ex-migrant laborers who are from the very poorest and most deprived areas of the rural South. These children must have education and are, therefore, enrolled in schools side by side with those privileged youngsters from very affluent and cultured homes.

This situation is insane! No one knows what to do. The Negro children from the rural South, who live in the school district, are by far weaker than migrants from the urban South, who at least have a fighting chance. Many of these rural Negro children, and their parents, come from school districts that are the very weakest in the South for either white or Negro; and here they are, side by side with the strongest among the entire nation. Obviously there must be no segregated institutions created under any guise to accommodate their need. That would merely accentuate the problem which is already at a critical state and the most difficult one facing northern school administrators. A very quick prescription is needed, but it is difficult to concoct. These young Negroes, in order to survive and succeed, will need every effort spent to help them overcome the impossible gap that exists between themselves and their more privileged white schoolmates. Incredible numbers of them drop out.

What is not clear, however, is why these youngsters are not permitted to go to school for the entire ten weeks in the summer in order that they may put in time-and-a-third to reckon with the critical lag from which they suffer. In other words, if a privileged Negro youngster or a privileged white youngster in Great Neck can get French III in nine months, why not start the underprivileged one with French III on June 15, as soon as the previous school year has closed, so that by the time September comes he has been dabbling in French III already for three months?

Who said that it was improper or illegal to run school the year round? One cannot see much warrant for these after-school endeavors for effective and immediate change when there stands before us the option of keeping some of these young people in school the year round. There could be teachers especially trained to work with them, to keep them on the main track, to keep them from dropping out, to keep them from being embarrassed by repeated failure, to keep them from seeing a classroom as a kind of cross on which to be crucified rather than a happy experience with other young people of the same age.

President Johnson has called for a teachers' corps. This idea is overdue. Just as the marines and paratroopers are equipped for special military missions, so we need teachers who are emotionally, intellectually, and morally equipped to take assignments among neglected and untaught children, to call them by name, love them with a whole heart, and draw smoke out of the computers that predicted that they could not be taught. Dr. Kenneth Clark declares that this is the heart of the problem:

To what extent are the contemporary social deprivation theories merely substituting notions of environmental immutability and fatalism for earlier notions of biologically determined educational unmodifiability? To what extent do these theories obscure more basic reasons for the educational retardation of lower-status children? To what extent do they offer acceptable and desired alibis for the educational default: the fact that these children, by and large, do not learn, is because they are not being taught effectively and they are not being taught because those who are charged with the responsibility of teaching them do not believe that they can learn, do not expect that they can learn, and do not act toward them in ways which help them to learn.[7]

Clark, a veteran hard bargainer in this area, goes further to allege that the IQ scores are mirages and the groupings that are so much in vogue are devices to exempt lazy and unimaginative teachers from difficult challenges. He says:

Many children are now systematically categorized, classified in groups labeled slow learners, trainables, untrainables, Track A, Track B, the "Pussycats," the "Bunnies," etc. But it all adds up to the fact that they are not being taught; and not being taught, they fail. They have a sense of personal humiliation and unworthiness. They react negatively and hostilely and aggressively to the educational process. They hate teachers, they hate schools, they hate anything that seems to impose upon them this denigration, because they are not being respected as human beings, because they are sacrificed in a machinery of efficiency and expendability, because their dignity and potential as human beings are being obscured and ignored in terms of educationally irrelevant factors—their manners, their speech, their dress, or their apparent disinterest.[8]

The whole matter of "grouping" young people according to intelligence quotients, reading levels, or other standards of readiness presents problems. No matter what device may be used, if a significant number of the children involved are Negro, then all the sediments of intellectual deprivation will settle among them and the division will amount to a racial grouping with all the ill effects now continuing with a new, professionalized legitimacy. What kind of education is it that one gets when he is aware of the fact that he and his Negro comrades are all given a special colony within the school, not because they are colored this time, but because they are less advanced intellectually?

There have been some startling results achieved in experimental programs which prove that the plight of the child who brings to school the deficiencies of ghetto culture is not an impossible condition.

The Northside Center for Child Development in New York

proved in remedial reading programs for one month during the summers of 1955 to 1964 that some children gained as much as two years in reading achievement and that the weakest ones gained five months.

In St. Louis, the Banneker Project under Dr. Samuel Shepard, proved that with intensive work the eighth-grade pupils moved from a deficit standing in reading ability of 7.7 years to 8.8 in thirty months. Also, the top among groups which began with only 7 per cent of the 16,000 pupils of the district grew to 22 per cent; the lowest track among the three shrank from 47.1 per cent of the total to 10.9 per cent.

Those who were part of that 15 per cent increase which climbed out of the bad statistics may be just digits on a graph to researchers, but they are real people who will be parents and whose children will have a very different starting point in life because the administration in St. Louis schools cared.

There is not yet sufficient evidence that a concerned citizenry is ready to work on any of these problems. The school administrators have to approach these problems with one hand tied behind them because there is not enough concern to support the efforts that they must put forth. This has to do with money, salaries, equipment, and the expenses for extra time offerings beyond the conventional school year. Moreover, it is doubtful that we shall produce enough teachers, with the necessary training and experience, to render the kind of service that deprived youngsters will need. The average teacher in Harlem today has less than two years' teaching experience. This is a big job to be attempted with rookies, and this is a terrible reflection of the level of concern. A much bigger effort than this will have to be made. No one can appreciate, for example, a teachers' union being so professionally encrusted as to oppose the assignment of the best teachers to the most demanding situations.

An Interim Strategy

The young Negro knows what is required to stop this cycle of ignorance from which he has emerged or within which he was trapped. He knows that all-Negro classes in any subject are suffocated by the stale and stifling hangover from the total Negro world of poverty and apathy. So he wants none of that. In his pristine innocence, he wants the whole system dropped and overhauled. He wants special help for those who find it hard to adjust to immediate transfers. He wants the dropouts saved. What he does not know is that others in town who resent the Negro advance, who are not enthusiastic at all about his gains, will not support these remedial programs, will fight a revised, increased budget, will fire a superintendent, will tell Negroes to get it the best way they can, and will get on the telephone to make converts.

There are "right-wingers" and "superpatriots" who associate the civil rights movement with "communism" and the emancipation of Negroes with the "red conspiracy." At bottom they are haters. They give ground only when they must. The school problem as it affects Negroes is their ball park, and they play hard. They know what the earliest segregationists knew; namely, that education liberates and ignorance perpetuates the long night of slavery.

This is the crucible. This is the test. Will our communities now pay the bill for rectifying a wrong so deliberately perpetrated against the Negroes? Will the invasion of the fascist-minded racists into the school arena put the responsible leadership to flight? Will corrective measures be devised, projected, and paid for, such as year-round schooling for those whose parents had their schools closed half the year for chopping cotton, curing tobacco, or picking a harvest of beans?

All the social awakening set in motion by the assertive leadership of the young Negro can bog down in weak training, poor performance, and the ongoing of the Negro stereotype if something is not done in terms of overcoming the educational deficits with such dramatic success that there will be some hope of catching up and keeping pace with the blinding speed of the acceleration in knowledge and in technology in American life. The sobering truth is that while we are talking about a deficit among Negroes, advances are being made on the educational front at such a pace that even those who suffer from no deficit at all, white or Negro, will have difficulty keeping the pace. The demands in terms of educational excellence are going to increase rather than level off.

It is nonsense to engage in empty talk regarding the responsibility of parents of socially disadvantaged children. Most of the parents of these youngsters are separated or divorced, the homes suffer from all forms of social bankruptcy, and there is no need to expect effective support from this type of family life. Yet the child did not ask to be born into this situation, and America cannot punish the child because of the accident of his birth. All of us need to assume a share of the guilt for having taken so long to correct racial patterns that the consequences of discrimination have grown to be so expensive. We shall have to pay our way out of this. Even at that, the price will be small compared to the cost that we are going to pay in welfare, penal institutions, rehabilitation centers, and all the cognate services that have to be rendered to those who become social parasites.

What the Government Is Doing About the Deficit

The President is giving exciting and determined leadership in this direction. Federal aid to education, the Elementary and Secondary Education Act of 1965, will offset much of the local lethargy and send the bigots whimpering to their dens. Those who fought federal aid were really fighting Negroes, straining every nerve to preserve their inferior status. If there is any doubt, check the views of opponents to Federal Aid to Education on other issues that would have likewise benefited Negroes.

The Higher Education Act included $30,000,000 for developing institutions, of which a sizable amount will improve the libraries, laboratories, exchange programs, extension offerings, and scholarship programs of the smaller Negro colleges. This is a beginning. With the federal partnership to foundations working in this area, some procedures will be found that will change the moral climate and eventually neutralize the color factor in education. Then watch all else change!

The federal establishment belongs in this field because, for one thing, it was a denial of basic constitutional rights for ninety years that created the educational lag. Private and church colleges were feebly standing up to a task that tax-supported institutions were performing for whites. Moreover, the nation can no more afford to let the Negro population continue to suffer from this educational deficit than it could afford yellow fever, unproductive farms, polluted water, or the indigent aged. In other words, it is a national problem too big and too urgent for piddling answers.

It will be worth the effort, for as we meet this challenge we shall learn much that will prepare us to face challenges at other levels. Any educational professional who dedicates himself to the discovery of solutions in this area will find himself growing as a psychologist, as a sociologist, as an administrator and as a counselor. His success in this area will merely prepare him for wider and larger professional service. If he can find a way to offset the general apathy of the profession toward the needs of Negroes, the answer will surely find applicability in helping others who are deficient for a variety of other reasons.

The Peace Corps has taught us this. Many persons who entered the Peace Corps with mediocre backgrounds came out having discovered a brand-new world, not necessarily in Africa or in Asia but in their own minds and hearts. They did not realize that so little of their brainpower and their moral energy had been used until they had to face the problems of adjusting to another culture, learning how to make adequate use of leisure time, searching for answers to critical questions regarding America's racial policies, and learning how to live with another Peace Corps volunteer from another section of the country who was the product of another style of living. Sargent Shriver demanded that they make these adjustments with the barest minimum of gadgetry and conveniences carted around the world to insulate them from such splendid opportunities. This concept left them standing body deep in the midst of humanity without Marshall Field, Gimbels, or Sears, Roebuck to save them. They found answers in their own untested resourcefulness.

So, whereas America spends one hundred million dollars to send ten thousand five hundred volunteers into forty-two countries, the returns that America will reap will be worth far more—excellent language teachers in Spanish and French, ambassadors and embassy staff members with far more savoir faire, and in much larger numbers, to staff the small posts around the world, new types of business executives for international operations who know how to speak the language and communicate with ease rather than stay hidden behind high walls sipping gin and tonic. Likewise, as we throw ourselves into the task of correcting the deficit in education among the Negroes, we are going to learn many things about education and human development that will help make the nation stronger on every hand.

One issue remains. As we reflect upon the emergency measures, the special catch-up efforts, the remedial programs, the foundation help and federal involvement, why is it that Dr. Otto Klineberg[9] did not find this yawning chasm between Negro and white academic achievement in New York in 1935? The young Negro needs to ask this of himself. Were Negroes brighter then? The answer is twofold. First, not all Negroes attempted high school then, and the migration to New York was not nearly so massive; it did not reach such a crescendo of rural people as we have today. Next, education is advancing; the demands are rising faster than the life of the Negro is improving. This is a serious warning to the young Negro. The gap is widening. Help is coming, but it is late. Time is unkind, and whatever is moving adversely is hurried by time. Thus the pressure is increased.

In practical terms, the young Negro will find himself outpointed and left behind, faced with utter disillusionment, when he discovers that his zeal for freedom and equality is cancelled out by his intellectual inadequacy to cope with the challenges that equality will impose upon him. It is one thing to make the demand for equality in terms of the highest ethical and political considerations conceivable. It is an even better thing to be able to stand alongside others knowing in one's heart and mind that the difference is only a matter of color and that in every detail of consequence there is equality in fact. The young Negro wants to be hastening toward that day when fewer and fewer explanations, apologies, and rationalizations need to be given for the disparities that yet remain, no matter where the responsibility lies.

This is a bitter truth, that in the final analysis this problem of educational deficits is a personal one. It may be described in a book or it may be crawling up a wall on a graph in the Office of Education, but it smacks the young Negro right in the face in a personnel office, in a dean's conference, or at a plant while he is taking a test in a lonely, quiet, small room. Therefore, it ceases at some point to be a major public issue and becomes very private indeed.

The Deficit As Faced by Some Young Negroes

In a random sampling of some young Negroes by letter, inquiring how they made it, the following excerpts from their replies are worth examination, as they reflect on the issue of overcoming educational deficits. Many have found the courage to take on the problem personally and carry in their hearts the burden of added challenge. Theodore Nims, Jr., salesman, General Electric Company, puts it this way:

"As a Negro, I feel I must put my best foot forward at all times. I must work not only with my white colleagues on the job, but in the community, as a participating citizen. This I feel is the steppingstone to a better tomorrow, and will make the burden easier for those who must follow."

Melvin E. Triplett, electrical engineer, Hughes Aircraft Corporation, found the gap facing him in military service; and he attributed it to his college courses:

"In my case, I became aware of the deficits of 'Negro' education throughout my tour of duty in the Army. During this time I was exposed to graduates of other schools and was able to make a comparison of the courses that I had completed and those that were required at other schools. Therefore, when I came out of the Army, I was resolved not to seek further education at a southern Negro school."

Weldon Jules, councilman, Ridgecrest, California, inherited his parents' concern for education, and this became his incentive to make it his goal to support the cause of Negro advance by becoming educated.

"The greatest single influence in my life that caused me to aspire towards the height I have now reached was my father's desire that all six of his children receive a college education. His words were, 'A Negro is unrecognized throughout the world without an education and especially in your hometown, New Orleans, Louisiana.' Consequently, I realized that in order to lead a decent life I must have a decent job and the only way to acquire a decent job is to be educated."

J. Mason Davis, attorney, Birmingham, Alabama, gives a typical case study of the problem, the full cycle from the early denial of opportunity, through the challenge of compensating in college, keeping pace with the students from more advantaged situations, and returning to live and serve as a leader in a city that still has yet to come to terms with the problem.

"The Negro public schools were woefully overcrowded. There were too many students in too few schools, with too few teachers. There was also the problem of having too many of the mentioned teachers who had received substandard instruction. This tended to produce an academic teaching vacuum. Added to the instances of poor teaching quality is the matter of overcrowded classes, some having 50 to 55 students. This allowed for little or no time for individual student problems. In my high school, there was no biology lab. The chemistry lab was too small for the students attending and there was little or no equipment. I never performed a chemistry experiment or one in the physics lab. This academic deficiency carried over to college where I found that it was necessary to study the first-year science course twice as much as the others to receive the grade A which I received in all other courses without too much difficulty. Talladega College, fortunately, presented none of the problems mentioned above. . . . My personal difficulty was experienced as a first-semester law student at the University of Buffalo where all of the students were white except for four Negroes. I experienced a period of adjustment to the new situation. It was at a point when all my classmates found that we came from divergent backgrounds but confronted a new and common problem, the study of law, that my period of adjustment ended and I found that my undergraduate studies had done a great deal in removing my prior deficiencies. . . . Finally, it is my belief that the Negro struggle for equality has caused me to cease thinking in terms of living and working in a Negro community."

H. T. Hutchins, Jr., associate professor of education, Albany State College, Georgia, gives witness again to the very private aspects of this problem. He was fortunate enough to be inspired by a dedicated teacher.

"The single greatest influence on my life which caused me to aspire toward greater heights was a high school teacher who took interest in me as a human being and not just another dirty kid from the Eastside. There were many academic shortcomings that I brought into adulthood out of 'Negro' education. The paramount deficit was in the area of oral and written communication."

Gilbert Ware, United States Commission on Civil Rights, Washington, D.C., reminds us of another aspect of the gap, the woeful lack of emphasis on the fine arts. The higher a Negro aspires to reach, the more apparent the crevices of weakness in his education are exposed to him.

"It is true that I emerged out of 'Negro' education with certain shortcomings, but I hasten to add that a sense of inferiority was not among these. I was aware of infirmities inherent in such education, but felt that many of them could be offset by diligence. This has proved to be the case, but there still exist deficiencies in several areas, not the least of which relate to an understanding and appreciation of art, music, literature, and languages. Throughout my graduate days at Princeton University, I had the disturbing feeling that I was a man who was trying to construct the thirteenth floor of an edifice while simultaneously endeavoring to complete the foundation. At times I am still troubled by this sensation, but self-improvement is merely difficult, not impossible, and I am closing the gap. The point of all this, of course, is that stronger educational underpinnings, established during my early years, would have done much to obviate this sort of 'filling in' operation, freeing me to carry out this function at a higher level of sophistication."

Hardy R. Franklin, Sr., community coordinator, Brooklyn Public Library, points up the detail that five of his high school English teachers were not even college graduates!

"I think that the greatest influence on my life was my mother. She stated very early the goals that she had in mind for her children. I think that the interest and concern of my brothers and sisters played a major role also in accomplishing our mother's wishes. This was also fortified by conditions that prevailed in my home town of Rome, Georgia. There was very little for the Negro to aspire towards. The educational opportunities were limited, the job opportunities, as you know, were very poor, the future of the Negro was limited and narrow, and the skills needed to survive under a segregated community were not really skills. The need for education was just beginning to be pushed. The Negro put little emphasis on education and the white community placed no emphasis on it for Negroes.

". . . there were deficits by virtue of the fact that I was a product of a separate and unequal school system. The most important being that the basic skills—the major portion of our education, were not taught correctly. I am speaking specifically of English grammar, vocabulary and literature, which was taught by teachers who were not sufficiently trained. To make it worse, there were no library facilities in school or community to supplement or allow for self-improvement. Upon entering Morehouse College, I was very disappointed when I scored low on the English test because I thought that this was one of my best subjects. Later I found that five of the teachers who taught me English from 7th through 12th grade, were not college graduates, nor were they English majors when they were students in college.

"We were always taught that we were just as good as the next man. The school or source of education was not as important as the application of the individual's training and knowledge to the situation or the environment in which he found himself. I firmly believe that the standards and goals set by parents, especially the mother, and the interest and devotion of teachers gave me the substance to move always towards the front. At all times, seeking, accepting challenges, being honest and sincere in endeavors and learning to take constructive criticisms gracefully were points to keep in mind. Of the four children in my family, two girls and two boys, all are college graduates. Three have Masters degrees, one of the three has almost completed the requirements for a Doctorate in English."

Daniel Grove, State Representative, House of Representatives, Denver, Colorado, points to that quality of courage and determination that covers the distance between what the young Negro has and what he wants.

". . . I performed duties as a Probation Counselor for the Juvenile Court, City and County of Denver, for the past eight years. Then finally at age 21, I married and, with two children plus buying a new home under the GI Bill of W W 2, I made up my mind that I was going to get all of the education possible under this bill. This firm decision was reached one morning in the fall of 1947 as I was riding along with several other Negro men in the rear of a pick-up truck, through the Campus of the University of Alabama. Our daily journey took us through the heart of that beautiful, lively and bustling campus. As we rode past many happy-appearing and eager students I then decided that I was going to pursue an education at all costs.

". . . I strongly feel that an educational deficit followed me into adulthood. This deficit, I feel, is the result of the system of 'Negro Education.' I do not place the blame on the many very dedicated and motivated Negro teachers, who, like myself, were deprived of a first class education. English and Math were the most obvious educational deficits that accompanied me into adulthood.

"I consider myself fortunate in that I had the opportunity to study at Stillman College, Tuscaloosa, Alabama. We, at Stillman, had a highly intelligent, well prepared, widely traveled, mixed faculty. This environment enabled me to rid myself of the long standing myth that members of certain racial groups are natively more intelligent and capable than the Negro. I am grateful for that experience and opportunity."

Don Anthony, plant buyer, The Kroger Company, Solon, Ohio, comes at this from another angle. He attended a "white" school and then discovered later that he had to take on the burden of the Negro stereotype and the price of discrimination in employment. His preparation for this challenge was made at Central State College under the eminent Charles Wesley.

"I guess in looking back at my childhood and early teens I'd have to say that athletic competition probably played the most significant part in influencing my future outlook on life. . . . I'll never forget sitting in the classroom in the seventh grade and listening to the 1947 world series being broadcast over the public address system. . . . I found that by participating in athletics both at the high school and college level there was a feeling of self-satisfaction that I obtained which at least partially compensated for the social inequities of being a Negro in an all-white institution.

"The neighborhood I live in is now about 99 per cent Negro with probably as high if not higher educational background (professional) than the white neighborhoods with homes in the same price range. It has been said that this neighborhood and even myself are not 'typical Negroes.' I have to laugh, particularly at work, when this is mentioned since I labored for two years doing unskilled work here until someone realized I wasn't 'typical.' If being given a chance to show my ability at work, live where I want and eat where I please is being typical then I guess we're all typical. . . . the initiative I had to exert to expand my horizons was to learn to have pride in being a Negro. It was not until I attended Central State College, Wilberforce, Ohio, that I was exposed to members of my race who had been taught about our race and role that we have played in this country's growth. People like Charles Drew, Paul Lawrence Dunbar and many others just don't appear in your textbooks."

Most enlightened Americans will become increasingly aware of the reasons for the deficits and will show concern. But it is not going to be healthy for the young Negro, emotionally and psychologically, to be making a stronger annual bid for full equality and then to have to add footnotes continually giving reasons for inability to perform on a strictly competitive basis. The samples above reflect the variety of problems and challenges that Negroes have faced in preparing for the types of employment that they must enter now in larger numbers. The single thread that runs through all these testimonials is that the burden of finding a remedy and getting ready had to be assumed by the victims themselves. No grand strategy was outlined for them that promised relief.

Therefore, the successful pursuit of intellectual achievement will have to rest largely on the individual who may have the common sense to observe that the penalty will be demanded in very private forms of suffering, such as denial of a job, limited social mobility, and a blurry-eyed view of the world around him that gets more complicated every day.

We may, and we shall, demand public and massive efforts. Many will be forthcoming. But the insatiable curiosity and the sense of adventure that start bells ringing in the soul and that create a mentally inquiring spirit are very personal acquisitions. They can be encouraged. But they cannot be conferred and they cannot be taken away. One should seek them, yes, for the sake of the advancement of his race, but they are more likely to be had for a cause that transcends race; namely, one's self-assurance that he has already defied the conditioning arrangement of inherited genes and that no matter what rumor has echoed down the corridors of centuries about his potentialities, these limits his own mind will explore, and their farthest extremities will be kept safely beyond any other human powers to establish or control.

In twenty years a great deal can happen. A Negro who was told in 1940 that he could not belong to a United States Navy band is now the bandmaster at Stewart Air Force Base at Newburgh, New York, and has been since 1960. Twenty years ago the Ku Klux Klan was threatening Thurgood Marshall as he appeared in southern courthouses presenting the case of the NAACP in salary equalization and graduate school admission cases. Today, if the government should have a case against the Klan, that same Thurgood Marshall, as Solicitor-General of the United States would devise the strategy for the government's case.

Twenty years is time enough for an unborn Negro to grow up, enter school, and graduate from a community college or a technical institute, or to reach his third year in college. That is our focus. What will he be like, what kind of education will he get? What kind of pace can the young Negro set, with all his weights and disabilities, so that 1980 will show far more progress than we saw from 1940 to 1960?

5

Breaking the Cycle of Poverty

LEARNING the technique and finding the strength to vault himself over the economic barrier will be the greatest test of the resolve of the young Negro, for nothing will resist him more persistently than the economic pressures in American life. The process of social change is pegged more closely to this slow movement from farmhand to industrial worker than to any other factor. Just as the present educational deficits of the American Negro have to be understood in terms of what happened in 1880 and 1890, likewise the economic status of the Negro traces back to his agrarian beginnings in the rural South.

The Economic Impasse

When a handsome, well-educated young Negro sits in a personnel office, waiting to present himself and his credentials to an interviewer, he grows tense as time sharpens his awareness of the fact that when his dark countenance bursts upon the rigid boundaries of racial consciousness in this white, middle-class mind, the whole panorama of American society and the place of the Negroes reels before him. The interviewer needs no signal. Either he will start looking for ways to conform, to deny the job, to stand by custom, to play it safe, or he will start out affirmatively, trying to find every way possible to keep from saying No. But he is forced to one side or the other of the issue, for the issue is there: namely, can an American white afford to open wide the door and let the Negro through the economic impasse? For once he traverses this sacred ground, then the correlation between crime, disease, ignorance, and a black face will surely begin to fade, and the Negro's color will become neutralized. Thus, each interviewer has to decide if he is for or against this process.

Is that what the prospective employer wants to happen? If it is, then he must assist the young Negro in scaling the walls that have shut him out of the inner workings of American economic life. When naïve whites question this premise and raise doubts regarding the Negro's capacity to appropriate an economic advantage, to manage well and to rise by economic successes, he has forgotten that the Negro never did have economic running space. A man of the first free generation of Negroes had no land and no capital, and did sharecropping. He had to give 40 per cent of his earnings to the man who owned the land and who had previously owned the workers. In most situations the sharecropper never saw the cash himself because the owner of the land sold him everything he needed at exorbitant prices and at criminal rates of interest. Thus, when the Negro looked at his remaining 60 per cent and saw what had to be paid for goods and services rendered—all provided by the "boss" and on his terms—his wages shrank to a pittance.

How could anyone save money, create capital, purchase equipment, and plan for expansion with this kind of exploitation? When he went into the city to work in the factory he was exploited again. When the tobacco factories sold a pound of select tobacco for $1 the labor cost on that was 5½ cents. In 1880 the wages paid the Negroes for labor in those factories was 80 cents a day for a sorter and 48 cents for a stripper.[1]

This situation still dogs the Negroes' tracks. Today there are two hundred counties in the seven Deep South states where most Negroes live in poverty-stricken condition. The migration to our northern urban centers from these counties is steady and it is likely to increase. Hence, the pathology of our northern urban communities remains an enigma unless there is a complete understanding of the origins of the persons who have migrated there and the depth of the poverty out of which they have come.

The Real Economic Status of the Negro

Many of the decision makers are confused because their Negro associates are far removed from this bottom in society. There are approximately six thousand Negroes in America who earned more than $25,000 in 1960. Those who observe these Negroes, who see their air-conditioned, split-level suburban homes, their finely manicured lawns and shrubs, who watch them throwing their golf bags into the trunks of their convertibles on Sunday morning, and teasing curious poor whites with their pretty wives and ready cash, taking off for Caribbean cruises, are likely to be deceived into believing that the plight of the Negro has changed more significantly than it really has. Indeed, there are those who have been able to escape patterns of discriminatory practices, to prepare themselves for the professions and jobs in industry that net high earnings, but the Negro people in general are suffering from the whole poverty complex that goes along with low incomes.

In 1959 over 1,200,000 Negro families earned under $2,000 per year, and nearly 1,500,000 others who earned more than $2,000 did not get up to $4,000. When you are making $60 per week in the United States, trying to support a family, you are poor. Make no mistake about that. By the time $20 of that goes for rent and $20 for food, there you have only $20 left for medical services, income taxes, recreation, clothing, utility bills, and assistance to other relatives who are not making even the $60 a week. For the more ambitious Negro father it means taking an extra job, working weekends and rendering himself, therefore, of even less value as a father, a partner in homemaking, a counselor to children, and a participating citizen in his community.

Herbert Bienstock, Bureau of Labor Statistics Regional Director in the Northeast, prepared a report on poverty in New York City in which the paradox of poverty against the backdrop of national affluence is sharply outlined. The report was made to the American Statistical Association, March 11, 1965.

According to the Bureau's accepted standard for minimal well-being, a family of four needed $6,353 a year to make it in 1960–1961. The government's poverty ceiling is $3,000. There are 317,000 families in New York City under the $3,000 income line. Among Puerto Ricans, 34 per cent of all families fall under the line and 27 per cent of all Negro families. This does not account for the majority of the number of families under this line, however; for 246,000 of the 317,000 families under the $3,000 line are white. It is highly significant that such a large percentage of Negro and Puerto Rican families are so poor in New York City. In fact, one out of every five Negro semiskilled workers earned less than $3,000 in 1960.

The Relation Between Poverty and Education

A part of the understanding of the problem is the relationship between poverty and education. In New York City, among young white males, ages 18 and 19, 47 out of every 100 are still in school; 29 of every 100 Negro young men are in school at that age. When one considers how many more whites than Negroes are counted in this category, the percentage is significant. Among those young men of ages 20 to 24 more than twice the percentage of whites are in school than Negroes.

When all males in New York City, ages 14 to 64, are accounted for, there are 154,000 who are not in school, not in jail, not in hospitals, not at work and not counted as unemployed. These are the young men who are at dead end in life and who demand our attention. These are largely the dropouts and 40 out of every 100 dropouts studied came from families of incomes less than $3,000. Thus, this poverty will pass from one generation to another.

Because of the fragile structure of a community of such poverty-ridden people, values that make for constructive citizenship are difficult to nurture and to embrace. One loses heart in trying to meet the standard of the ideal person against which he is measured. Such goals seem unattainable when the basic, elementary goals of survival are difficult to reach. It is therefore not too hard to understand the patterns of social disorganization and the large number of fatherless households. And, when the father is not present and earning, the family income goes down to hopeless margins of survival. In those lowest income brackets, of course, there is the highest percentage of homes without fathers present. Where incomes are highest, there are more fathers present. This is just one of the highly determinative social factors related to income.

The young Negro, with a heart full of zeal and his mind conditioned by a clear-cut, logical analysis of the condition of his people, runs head-on into this cycle of cause and effect that is so pervasive in our society. His initial zeal and the enthusiasm that accompanied his sit-ins and the marches will have to be transformed into a stubborn staying power that will keep him toe to toe with the tricky problems of advancement until he begins to see dawn break after this long night of economic deprivation. Again, every criterion by which he is measured compels him to bow to the relationship between poverty and the gloomy statistics that are held before him in bold relief.

How Poverty Reinforces an Inferior Status

The ways in which poverty effectively guarantees an inferior status for the Negro people are innumerable. *First,* when you are poor you have to live in a dirty, crime-ridden community, a swampland of human waste breeding every type of social deviate. You have to live in a section of the city which has been abandoned by four or five waves of European migrants and abandoned finally by the middle-class Negroes. Because the people are poor and without influence, the streets are the last ones to get swept, building codes are the last to be enforced, and police protection is perfunctory and often with the abuse of those who live there. When the agents of the city do not care, and when the police are indifferent, dope peddling, prostitution, violence, and every form of personal decay continue without interruption. Then watch these statistics accumulate, and watch the sociologists have a field day. The bigots pile up ammunition.

Second, the type of leisure available to the dwellers of the slums helps to mold them into problem personalities. The taverns and beer joints are on every corner magnetizing the lowest elements of society. The music that is heard from the juke boxes evokes the most emotional type of response. Gambling for kicks and gambling for rent are commonplace. The grassy parks and the marble libraries are located in other sections of the city and require an expenditure of energy, of pride, and of money to reach. And when one knows that he is not expected and not wanted in those other sections of town, he is not likely to roam in those parts.

Third, look at the circle of friends who gather, look at the other personalities that are populating the slum and the next apartment, and see what little hope there is for these victims to help each other. They are all suffocating together. Leadership for Boy Scout troops, for YMCA groups, for the PTA is hard to come by, and the slum dwellers have to depend on each other for inspiration. The pastor of the local church is an import from the culture of the rural South, often poorly trained, and without urban orientation.

Fourth, look at what happens to children in this condition. What does a young girl come to believe about herself when on every Friday and Saturday night middle-aged, neurotic white and Negro men circle around her neighborhood looking for a young prostitute. When a young girl is approached a half-dozen times a week by teen-agers, married men, and pimps, what conclusion does she come to about herself, about the worthwhileness of life and about what the world expects of her? It is a miracle when a girl is able to climb out of the slum without an illegitimate child. When the young people see full-grown Negro men sitting around all week long unemployed and disengaged in any constructive way, what conclusion do they reach about their opportunities in life? How much inspiration does a young Negro boy get from this scenery to encourage him to learn well his algebra, French, American history and biology, to prepare for admission to a technical institute so that one day he can work for Westinghouse? He does not believe that any of this makes sense.

Fifth, those who do try to improve themselves and who seek the better things in life discover how much the entire community is conspiring against them. For example, when they go to buy a secondhand automobile they discover that because they live in that neighborhood the insurance rates are higher and the interest rate on the loan is higher. A prescription costs as much as ten times more in the ghetto pharmacy than it does in the upper middle-class neighborhood. Everything costs as much as two or three times more than what is charged a middle-class Negro who can protect himself or one who happens to be white.

Sixth, exploitation in interest rates is only one form of vulnerability the slum dwellers must endure. At election time, the local politician comes through, promising everything, encouraging them to support him for office; and, looking to this as one possible hope, they sell themselves once again and find nothing changed.

Seventh, consider what happens in terms of long-range planning, the kind of scheming that middle-class families can do, looking forward to the creation of some capital, a retirement with something beyond the barest necessities available, or putting aside something for the education of children. When one is poor, he stands with his nose against the wall of extinction; and the benefits of long-range planning and reasonable insurance rates are not available to him. He cannot project himself into the future when his present situation is so tenuous.

Eighth, consider how long the poor will go without medical care, with gnawing pains in the abdomen, seeing black spots before their eyes, getting tired in the middle of the afternoon without a known cause. Look at how susceptible they are to quack remedies, fortune tellers, and faith healers because they do not have the money to get adequate medical care from reliable and professional practitioners.

Ninth, note how you lose the respect of everyone when you have to write down a known slum address on a form, in school, or even in church. One becomes accustomed to thinking of himself as a person without caste. And once he is convinced of that, he acts accordingly and the statistics pile up. The sociologists send the dotted line crawling up the graph paper.

Tenth, a report on *Southern Justice: An Indictment*[2] shows another condition facing the poor that is often overlooked. A Negro convicted in a traffic court for driving without his license was fined $25 or sentenced to four months in prison. He did not have $25 and he had to accept the prison term. Another was sentenced to a $35 fine or twelve months in jail for public drunkenness! Thus, when you are poor you are caged, trapped, and defenseless.

It will take all the muscle and imagination that this vanguard of young Negroes can command to continue to make successes against these pervasive, persistent, and penetrating negative social forces. It is much simpler to integrate a library, a swimming pool, or a hamburger stand. Transforming the cities' slums, and rescuing those who perish there, will take more than the courage to demonstrate, and certainly more than impulsive showmanship. This will separate the sheep from the goats. There was a quality of novelty and excitement that gave momentum to those early demonstrations and swept up in the movement many who may not possess the discipline to follow through in this next crucial phase. But the young Negro who meant business is called to do nothing less than to ready himself and multiply his forces for this engagement, for if it is equality that he struck out for in 1960 when he broke ranks with his more conservative adult contemporaries, he must not weaken when he discovers that significant change yet remains to be made, and that it comes hard. The surface has just been scratched. The task will not allow for divisiveness, and he must develop more respect for some of the sincere old-timers who were inhibited by their doubts that demonstrations would help. Many old-timers have changed now, and for the long-range operations the young Negro will need every ally that he can find.

The Middle-Class Negro

The young Negro militants do not feel that the time has yet arrived for such a rapprochement with the Negro and/or white middle class. They argue that the "message" has not yet been heard and that there is still nothing waiting for them at the conference table but a polysyllabic "snow job." They do not understand the Negro power group, the professionals, the educators, the "in" politicians, the administrators. This group of middle-class Negroes comprises those who were in college during the depression years, who waited tables, hauled ice, shined shoes, washed cars, wrote numbers, sold whiskey, hopped bells, hustled baggage, and nursed white children to make it. They see nothing wrong with success. They are proud to own nice homes, send children to prep schools, sit on boards of trustees, control churches, and contribute to good causes. They are not revolutionaries. They would be faking if they tried to speak the jargon of revolution. They acquired the discipline to wiggle and sweat their way from a peanut farm to a federal judgeship, from a Memphis shanty to Westchester, and from a shoeshine box to vacations in the Bahamas.

These middle-class Negroes know the route from poverty to adequacy, from squalor to comfort, from ignorance to enlightenment. They look upon the young militant as an excessive opportunist who would rather talk than work. They do not see in the ranks of the militants those who have hitched themselves to a tough job and stayed with it, pulling it through economic vicissitudes, solving tangled problems, and meeting payrolls. They have great contempt, therefore, for those who seek to criticize the Negro middle class and to create an estrangement between it and the Negro masses.

They have a suspicion that the roles in which they are cast are more a matter of simple jealousy than anything else. They feel that the status that they have won is deserved, earned, paid for in blood, and not to be sacrificed for unemployed dropouts or wide-eyed young demagogues. Their point is that they represent what the young Negro should be fighting for, the inclusion of black folk in the inner circle, the possibility of a black man having some money and some power and some fun. If every black man who "arrives" must then start ducking the darts of the young warriors, what is the battle for, anyway?

But the young militant does not really object to affluent Negroes having money, fun, and power. It is their indifference to those who are trapped in poverty, their moral snobbishness in ascribing the term "lazy" and the appellation "hoodlum" to all the unemployed Negro males when the most casual glance at the evidence proves that they were never really encouraged to prepare, never convinced that jobs were possible, never privileged to live around those who walked toward the future, chest out, chin in, and full stride ahead.

The blind spot before the eyes of the Negro middle class is their unawareness that they left a mighty host behind in those slums when they crawled out. There was not room for many on the ladder to success in the forties, and only a few made it. Moreover, the present situation obviously is not answered by fratracide among Negroes, but by a united effort, a pooling of resources and a common front. Thus, it is time for the young militants to admit that they have no real program and for the middle class to admit that their social position is a curse to them if they fail to reach down and lift.

White and Negro Power Structures

The cycle of poverty will not be broken unless young militants, who do not have lower Manhattan offices, who are not saving for Bahaman vacations, who are not paying prep school bills, do continue to sound off and shake the indifference and callousness out of the business community. It will not be broken by that action alone, however. It will take the "establishment" in business, politics, religion, education, and labor to make changes and open doors to young Negroes, to drop the token technique and to begin a program for a massive effort in training, employment, and upgrading, and for the inclusion of Negroes in supervision and management.

It seems that there is really no way to avoid the "establishment" or the "white power structure" and its black satellites if things are ever going to move. After all, the power in housing, education, manufacturing, philanthropy, government, religion, commerce—or whatever—is there, in control and deeply entrenched. The Negroes who do have decent jobs, who have stormed the poverty barrier and moved it, work for, with, and under the agents of power.

Where these agents of power, Negro and white, have not "gotten the message" it will take massive and convincing protests, marches, sit-ins, and the works. But where the message is known, felt, heard, and where response is ready, the atmosphere of hostility and the rigidity of a posture of antipower is nonsense. This turns means into ends, confuses the issues and stalemates real progress. At least the agents of power should be given the even chance to prove earnestness if for no other reason than to give them an opportunity to burn off the tar of guilt and to make conciliation possible.

An unrelenting campaign of alienation and heated indictment, with no ventilating gestures at all, grouping all agents of power in one oblong mass, polarizes the situation, crystallizes intransigence, gives new reasons for stubbornness, brings the whole issue closer and closer to bloodshed, violence, and death instead of jobs, change, opportunity, and the open society.

Five years ago it was quite different. Then one could assume that big business, universities, foundations, and the leaders of government had taken Negroes for granted. There are too many who still do. But most do not today, and with responsiveness on the part of the young Negro things can move.

Before 1960, it was true that the "old line" Negro civil rights organizations were too accommodating, but the young Negro has stiffened these groups and has changed their program objectives.

The New Importance of the National Urban League

Let us look at an organization like the National Urban League, for example, with branch chapters in cities throughout the United States, and examine its role in this process. An effective Urban League branch says this to a local community: (1) Here are some recent and accurate facts and figures about your town that you may not have known, that have been gathered and interpreted by trained professionals. Look at them and tell us what you think. (2) This Urban League goes further to say that the facts, though incredibly alarming, need not remain unchanged. (3) It goes on to say, We shall gather the most concerned, the most talented, and the most dedicated people that we can find, white and Negro, to work together to find out what resources there are available in this community to effect change. (4) When we find ways of operating and run into the need for legislation, we shall then launch a program of education for legislation. (5) When we discover corruption in the political structure, we shall start holding meetings, forums, and discussions to expose this corruption. (6) When the CORE or SNCC shock troopers come to town and frighten the power structure to death, lying down in the City Hall and picketing the police station, and leave, this League remains here on a continuing basis, ready to channel this new concern, this fresh awareness quickened by this CORE or SNCC strategy into immediate, constructive programs that must be picked up at the level of local leadership when the SNCC and CORE invaders have moved on to shake up the next town. (7) We shall publish our activities, our successes, and our failures and share them with other communities around the country. (8) Government agencies will talk with us, and much of what we shall have found workable will seep into new legislation and will raise the challenge to a higher and more hopeful synthesis the next year, and the next.

The pity is that an organization like this has been so poorly supported over so long a period, and the unique contribution that the young Negro has made to the Urban League is that he has compelled the business world to look for a new way of meeting the Negro challenge without having to deal with the young Negro in the streets. And, as management has looked around to find a constructive way of approaching this problem, it has discovered the Urban League standing there, neglected. With the dynamic

Whitney Young heading the League, building on the foundations laid by Eugene Kinkle Jones and Lester Granger over the long years when money and initiative were both scarce, this organization appears to be the kind that is needed for these years during which the young Negro must transpose his initiative from drama to the sustained drive for lasting gains.

In 1964, 271 major corporations contributed to the Urban League. In 1963, the year before, 181 contributed. There were 68 new contributors in 1964. In 1963 there were 49 new contributors over 1962. These are largely Americans who insist that social changes must be made through private, rather than governmental, means. Really, what many Americans mean by this is that changes should not be made at all, for when change is left up to private resources, it is usually a guarantee that it will be *left,* period. But there are those today in growing numbers who are serious about change now and who would like to see the private resources of this country applied to these problems. They should find the Urban League a strong resource already oriented toward the business and industrial community, in need of broader based mass support and more contact with the "poor," to be sure, but advantageously nationally structured and prepared morally to repair its middle-class image to meet the new challenges that the present developments have unfolded.

Varieties of Strategies and Personalities

Though the Urban League has a special appeal to the business community, with its twice and thrice degreed, Ivy League clad, social worker types and the soft-voiced, dry Martini-at-four sessions, the young Negro is correct in his suspicion that this approach alone is insufficient. The best intentions of management get stymied in the foot dragging of supervisors, the hypocrisy of unions, and the atmospherics of public opinion. Will whites fly in a commercial plane piloted by a Negro, decorated, Air Force veteran pilot of twenty years service in all types of aircraft? Will clients buy big policies from a Negro agent of a front-line insurance company? Will the contractor deal with a Negro architect on a $10,000,000 project? Will the orchestra quit if we hire a Negro conductor? Such questions get hung up in the minutes of boards of directors for months, and the young Negro waits.

These real issues are in the area of delicate and nondescript recesses in human nature. Action gets bogged down in something close to Original Sin. Are known advantages ever surrendered voluntarily? How soon and in what proportions? Surely here and there, now and then, a pioneer effort may be found and celebrated. But unless the NAACP prods the Justice Department into doing something about discrimination in unions through the courts, and until the brand-name manufacturers start getting sensitive about selective buying practices, and until it becomes a part of the American fair play syndrome of public reaction to give a break to an applicant from the minority communities, the discussion stage of equal job opportunity will whine and dine on and on. The changes that have come about were in *response* to management *responding* to the government's *response* to the impatient young Negro since 1960.

The efficacy of the young Negro's protest, therefore, may be seen at four points in the process of breaking the cycle of poverty:

1. He has already dramatized economic injustices to the extent that strong moral leadership has come from the White House and from management in responding.
2. He has encouraged a revival of the Urban League nationally, and the creation of other massive efforts that promise change in the patterns of economic opportunity.
3. He has given new significance to the legal thrust of the NAACP against illegal discrimination in unions, in voting rights, among government contractors, in government agencies, and in violation of fair employment laws.
4. He has challenged the apostles of discussion to prove that economic changes would have come about without his aggressive moves.

Of course, organizations like SCLC and Martin Luther King, CORE and James Farmer, and SNCC and John Lewis, as compared to the Urban League and the NAACP, believe in direct personal involvement. They can hope for only the most liberal white support—much of which will be limited—and anonymous and occasional, temperamental Negro support. When the issues are joined and enthusiasm is high, they can get white and black money and action. But most Negroes have such problems in their personal struggles for security that they have neither taken the time nor given the thought to the matter of aligning themselves with one of these direct action programs or another.

It seems paradoxical that organizations like SCLC, CORE, and SNCC that have played such an important role in harnessing the indignation, exposing the hurt, and revealing the courage of the Negro people are so ineffective when it comes to diagraming a long-term strategy that promises real change in the life of the Negro. They have not succeeded in developing strong local bases. Their leaders are megaphone, microphone men—not desk and chair, door-to-door, telephone (local!), lapel-holding, typing, mimeographing wheel horses. Everyone is an embryonic Dr. King!

Just as victories must be won on many fronts, so the varieties of strategies will involve many different types of personalities. We needed a sharp lawyer like Thurgood Marshall as well as a thundering, platform analyst like Mordecai Johnson; a bold field general like James Farmer and veteran inside men like Julius A. Thomas, William J. Trent, and J. Oscar Lee; we had to have Dr. King, but to keep more Dr. Kings coming we needed men like Dr. Benjamin Mays, Dr. Steven Wright, and Dr. J. M. Ellison; we need Whitney Young to stay on the banquet-conference circuit, but when the corporations start looking for Negroes to take the jobs that Young says we must have, we had better be grateful for men like Foster of Tuskegee, Troup of Fort Valley, Brawley and Clement of Atlanta, "Brud" Holland of Hampton, Samuel Duncan of Salisbury, Hollis Price of Memphis, Albert Dent of New Orleans, Felton Clark of Baton Rouge and a score of other educators who have to do the leg work of finding the teachers, the money, and the equipment to train the more than 100,000 Negroes now in colleges in the South. When Thurgood Marshall and Roy Wilkins won a Supreme Court victory, it was the work of men like Charles Johnson, Charles Wesley, Lester Granger, St. Clair Drake, W. E. B. DuBois, Kenneth Clark, E. Franklin Frazier, Allison Davis, John Hope Franklin, and Horace Bond that must be credited, those who updated the racial debate at the crucial point in every decade, set the new points of reference, stimulated discussion in educational, legal, and political science circles, dug out the facts, marshaled the ideas, wrote the articles, and briefed the legal warriors to go marching around the Jericho wall of segregation until it fell! Yet who could say that the yeoman service of A. Philip Randolph was of greater or less importance than the scholarly, oratorical brilliance of Charles Wesley? The millions of whites who have heard Mordecai Johnson, Benjamin Mays, and Howard Thurman over the past thirty years are now represented in every important forum on what must be done to build this city with solid foundations.

So, as we move into a new phase of the Negro struggle, the young Negro must be able to see that the work already done has been a prelude to something else, the tedium of co-operating with bread-and-butter programs. This is not going to create headlines, promote specialists in public address or TV personalities. The task is to break the logjam of ignorance and poverty and get the color factor neutralized in American life. Thus, in order to break the cycle of poverty and to vault himself out of economic despair, the young Negro will discover that new strategies and new techniques will have to be engaged, and this will involve aligning himself with large programs and massive efforts that go far beyond the kind of dramatic demonstrations that brought him to the forefront.

The awful possibility that talented, middle-class Negroes who have escaped the poverty cycle may hide in the shrubs of the suburbs and nonchalantly circle past the ghettos on the expressways to their carpeted, downtown offices is frightening, for their leadership can make the critical difference. Instead of becoming buffers and mufflers, hiding people from each other and drowning important voices, they should become ushers and amplifiers, bringing people together and making voices heard.

The awful possibility that business and government may miss the point, pass out more highly visible, ineffective, ornamental appointments, seek to anesthetize the protest movement with clever, tranquillizing gestures, and leave the main issues untouched is even more frightening. The young Negro is not stupid. Transparent tokens will only insult the movement and make even more difficult any rapprochement with agents of power and lengthen the days of tension.

The Imperative of Bigness on All Sides

There must be bigness on all sides, on the part of the educated, well-placed Negro, the policy makers in business and government, and the leadership in protest movements. Old power games that were played in city after city, in which the object was to see how much noise and movement could be made without changing anything are over. The explosions in Watts, Harlem, Paterson, Rochester, and Chicago have required a new beginning.

There is no way for the young militant to enjoy moral sterility while everyone who has decisions to make and consequences to live with must sully his conscience with the grime of compromise. The agents of power are responsible to boards, stockholders, auditors, laws, precedents, and public opinion. It is true that an effective public demonstration indeed moves all these inhibiting forces to new positions, but at whatever point in time the agent acts, he must do so within this broad frame of reference. The young militant indeed hastens the day for action, but when the day comes he must be ready and willing to sit down and admit the given factors that must be lived with and do business.

We are concerned now with jobs, apprenticeships, promotions, and new positions at the top. We are taking a close look at that hiatus between those who are managers and economic policy makers and those who are demanding change. When these two forces are eased together and each point of view becomes clearer, the focus should be on the problem, the opportunity; the new opening, the new jobs, the new hope, the status won—not on who lost face, who gave ground, or who surrendered. The winners should be the poor folk who need jobs, children who need eyeglasses, infants who need nutrition, families who need decent housing, fathers who need better jobs, and communities that need "beauty for ashes, the oil of joy for mourning, and the garment of praise for the spirit of heaviness."

This discussion means nothing to those who have turned the corner in their thinking, who have given up on "whitey," and who feel that only a full-scale revolution has relevance. The message presented here is for those who are angry, who are not yet convinced that a revolution is sane or possible, who want results now but who need to be assured that the atmosphere for change is here! This is *today,* not 1925 or 1945. And a rigidity on both sides about doctrinal approaches to change will delay important progress that should proceed now.

In addition to (a) the concern generated within the Negro community, (b) the efforts of foundations and corporations, (c) the programs of government in encouraging equal opportunity on a volunteer basis and enforcing compliance where the law is already clear, a new climate of opinion must be established in the country regarding the poor, especially the Negro, Puerto Rican, Mexican and Indian poor, the people who have traditionally been assigned to the lowest rungs of the economic ladder. It is gratifying to see the efforts being set forth today by the poverty program, which will have as much value in establishing a new climate of opinion as it will in accomplishing genuine successes in the lives of those it seeks to help directly. It is gratifying, also, to see how the National Council of Churches has disturbed the American Protestant community and exposed its lethargy and timidity. If Protestant leadership can be aroused, this will go a long way, for so many of the causes of discrimination are rooted in institutions controlled by the established Anglo-Saxon Protestant segments of business leadership. This is not to gainsay efforts made by the Catholic and Jewish communities, but it is important to emphasize the significant changes that could be made if the Protestants should succeed in giving leadership toward a new understanding of the moral indictment that rests upon the nation for permitting poverty to remain so long-term in the lives of so many people.

Most whites are unmoved by sentimental arguments to help the poor because they have been reared in a culture in which it has been implicit that the healthiest economy permits hard-working, inventive people to make all the money that they can. The spillover from their economic gains, the theory implies, would help the poor. This is a very naïve view because it takes into account only a segment of the problem. It gives no attention at all to discriminatory practices on the basis of color, to deliberate impediments placed in the path of those who are Negro or who belong to other despised and rejected groups. These whites want the laissez-faire atmosphere to prevail for themselves, but they allow the atmosphere to be fogged with prejudice and discriminatory treatment for others. This attitude does not take into account the view which hangs over from slavery that a Negro does not need very much and therefore should not demand so much. President Franklin D. Roosevelt ran into a storm of protests over the wages paid Negroes under the Works Progress Administration. There were those who could not swallow the notion that a Negro should be paid the same amount that a white man was paid, even though both of them were on relief programs established by the federal government. When the Negroes tried to change their condition in the late 1880's by organizing a Colored Farmers Alliance, the white farmers fought the movement. They admonished the Negroes not to be confused by these "side issues" and to look to religion and "see the glory of the Lord."[3]

The Common Cause of Negroes and Poor Whites

Such attitudes have prevailed in absolute incongruity to the prevailing American dogma that a man should work hard and prove his right to economic blessings. Not only is there this notion that the Negro should not have very much, but the concomitant to this is to confuse the poor white man by telling him that Negro agitation is really a design to elbow the Negroes up to an economic level beyond his own. This encourages the poor whites to meet in fields burning crosses, to fire their pastor when he talks about brotherhood, to chase around shooting Negro leaders, burning churches, and calling the federal government an instrument of creeping socialism. They do not realize that the same attitudes that keep the Negro in poverty will keep them close to poverty also. The poor white man has been anesthetized by the mischievous concept that no matter how bad his plight is he is still better off than the Negro. Since he dissipates his energies fighting the Negro, he has cultivated no advocate for his needs anywhere. Even when he decided to organize protest groups, they were groups protesting against the Negroes rather than against his own social plight and his own economic deprivation. In fact, his new interest in demonstrations is merely a reaction to Negro advances.

One outstanding exception is the organization of the Council of the Southern Mountains. In forty-four counties of eastern Kentucky one-half of the population receives some form of public aid. The Council aids migrants from this area in enabling an adjustment in their new urban surroundings in Chicago and other centers. Volunteers are recruited to go to the area for community development projects and health education and to bring cultural and educational enrichment. This is a new organization.

Indeed, in the long run, the poor white may discover that the aggressive young Negro whom he has despised was his unwitting ally. For when the Negroes really begin to move and make substantial gains economically and politically, the poor white rabble-rouser will discover himself to be haranguing before a smaller and smaller crowd of poorer and poorer people. The self-respecting poor white will send his son to the State Teachers College and the technical institute where he will rub shoulders with his Negro buddies and discover common cause in making America a great nation for everyone. He will see nothing to be gained by spending his time fighting people who are trying to help themselves.

Poverty as a Permanent Status

Every influence that can be brought to bear against the prevailing notion that some people should remain poor should be a welcomed one. The moral climate of opinion regarding the poor must change both for the Negro and the forgotten poor white.

The war against poverty must brace itself for attacks on both its right and left flanks. On the right there are arguments that efforts to change the status of the poor are purely politically motivated, a reward for the Negro vote and a bid for enlarged support. The argument continues that the poor are a part of an endemic human condition, like sin, flat feet or red hair. It will be here after billions of wasted dollars and mountains of staff reports. Comfortable people find it hard to empathize with the poor, and when "right-wing" political propaganda is added to natural drives toward self-preservation, there is little surprise that the anti-poverty program will be opposed by those whose ego requirement calls for a mass of the permanent poor to look down upon. Any threat that creeping egalitarianism will eliminate this social bottom is as frightening as walking trees or flying saucers. It is an omen of class destruction and, hence, self-liquidation.

It is understandable, therefore, that those who already find it hard to compete will never welcome the rising up of another 35 million Americans out of the pit of poverty to demand jobs, housing, recreation and adequate health facilities. Politically, this fear will congeal into a rigid posture of resistance to any efforts put forth to create effective change in the plight of the poor.

On the left, there are growing numbers of the estranged whites and Negroes who have given up on traditional modes of amelioration, who feel that the power elite are too deeply entrenched, who are cynical about all existing political structures and who are determined that nothing like school desegregation, anti-poverty programs or urban renewal will be given any chance for success. They work for chaos. They seek stalemates. They call every Negro with a steady job an "Uncle Tom." They have no dialogue with SNCC, CORE, SCLC or the NAACP. They gave up on the Urban League a long time ago. All nonviolent approaches are to them "sissy" accommodationist approaches that will legitimize the perpetual exploitation of the weak. Whether they are actually Communists or not, the intellectual stance of these left-wing habitués is just as alien to free institutions. That is, they do not count on change coming about by choice but by a violent transition. They have seen only a tiny fraction of the Negro poor involved in civil rights activity. They theorize that the remaining masses of the discontented ones are waiting for another type of program of social change that will really change things.

More and more young Negroes are being exposed to their point of view, for as their frustrations deepen and the intransigence stiffens, this argument becomes more and more plausible.

There is little that discussion and debate can do to dissipate this stolid disillusionment. It thrives on literature from revolutionary intellectual colonies and other publications from all over the world; it is strengthened by intractable white power, the monumental United States' slums, the lukewarm response to the President's appeals for equal employment practices and the indifference of the Negro elite. No verbosity will be sufficient in the face of this. What will work? Successful change will! The evidence that American institutions have the vitality, the self-correcting devices and the moral capacity to make quick change will cause such a campaign to lose credibility.

The multi-faceted anti-poverty program is the latest and broadest gauged instrument of change, and it must defeat the cynics and succeed.

Every community that spends more time and effort scheming to keep the poor out of anti-poverty policy-making and planning than it does on devising methods for assuring their inclusion merely confirms what the cynics have alleged, undermines the President's intent and invites the poor to look to leadership outside established channels for support. And, the one thing that the war on poverty was designed to accomplish was the creation of a meaningful and constructive vehicle to convey the ideas and aspirations of the poor.

Assuming that the Negro militants and the agents of power may find a way of responding to each other, that the total front of Negro organizations may move without fragmentation, that the white Protestant business community may take a stronger initiative and that the poor white may make common cause with the Negro poor, what remains?

There remains the task of cultivating within the mind of the young Negro an understanding of what is expected, what is demanded, what constitutes job success, and what the rewards can be. The poverty cycle will not break with the mere relaxing of discriminating practices. There is more to it than that. There has to be individual success, individual movement, individual advancement. Given the lag, a great deal of success is going to be required; and, in order for this to come about, the young Negro, who has had up to now very poor job orientation, will need help in understanding his new role, his new opportunity.

In addition to his inner fears, his understandable suspicions, and his cautious acceptance of a new role, the young Negro is aware of the stares of his fellow workers, the long delay in taking him on, the special preparations made for him and the guessing about his chances to make good. He also knows that the burden of a dark face will always call for an extra push.

When the Irish and Eastern European immigrants came to the United States they were white. They did not have to fight the persecution that went along with being a Negro. They could afford to go on and buy a cart of lemons, pick up a sledge hammer and start working on the railroads, or start lifting freight on the wharf, because they had not been robbed of their basic selfhood by being considered something close to plant life. They knew also that with a few dollars, a Brooklyn accent, a decent job, a shave, a shoe-shine, and a new suit they could move on into society. No one would ever stop them to read the immigration papers in their wallets to see how long they had been here or what kind of work they did. But a Negro could never rub the black from his face, nor could he rub from the minds of those about him the stereotypes that they continued to embrace. Therefore, the Negro's problem in working himself into a new role, approaching a new status, will require much understanding until the stereotype fades and color itself no longer remains an absolute index to personal acceptance.

The Challenge in Job Preparation Today

The corollary to the drive the young Negro made in reminding America of the injustices against him must now be matched by a campaign within his own ranks to cultivate sophistication about the quality of work that will get him into the best jobs, keep him there, guarantee his promotion and bring him to income levels that will permit him to put a few dollars aside and become part of those who own and guide the American financial establishment. This is as important as anything that government programs, lawsuits, and protests will do, but it is not—it bears repeating—a substitute for government action, court victories, and protests.

This is not easy, for the kinds of jobs that young Negroes have had and the kinds of jobs that their parents have had were different from the kind they must get. These old jobs involved oral instructions, a white man or an executive white woman giving orders with a staccato voice and a finger pointing. The orders were given orally, and the mistakes were not dead serious. In these jobs mistakes could be corrected easily. There was hour by hour supervision less than ten yards distant. If one did not show up for work the supervisor could do the job or he could pull someone in off the streets to do it in a hurry. No training was necessary except to stand still and listen until you heard it right. One worked with others just like himself so that there was no orientation to new and strange mores among one's fellow workers. Excellence was quickly attainable, the competition was weak, standards for success were fuzzy and poorly defined, and the job paid very little money.

The kinds of jobs that the young Negroes want, that pay good money and offer greater security, are entirely different. They begin with written instructions, and one has to study nights. There is little time to hang around the bar and listen to old jokes. It means being called an egghead or "a square" or something worse as one goes home and studies his instructions and manuals. Again, these jobs into which Negroes must move in much larger numbers do not permit costly mistakes. Dropping a tray in a restaurant or spilling coffee on a guest can easily be corrected. But miscalculating the trajectory of a missile or using a wrong formula in establishing production costs can send an error whizzing through a war or fouling up a multimillion dollar contract. Supervision is present, but remote; and no one stands humped over an electronics engineer or a pharmaceutical research chemist.

Next, replacements are difficult to find and considerable investment is made in the training for such jobs. Therefore, a measure of seriousness must accompany the entire process of job orientation. There are few things to joke about, and sustained periods of concentration will be required. The persons selected for such jobs come from wide recruiting efforts that cover the entire country, and a Negro from Boston's Roxbury section may be working alongside a California citizen of Japanese ancestry. A Negro from South Carolina may be working beside a Minnesota recruit who has never gone to school with a Negro and has heard only rumors about the civil rights struggle. One has to be cosmopolitan enough to establish quick and easy rapport with persons of widely different backgrounds. Competition will be keen, and one cannot expect to walk away with applause after an early, successful adjustment. One should not be waiting for high praise for normal and minimal success. This is not part of the pay as it was on those older types of "colored" jobs. Standards in these types of jobs are established on the basis of scientific criteria. One cannot trade congeniality for excellence in these new types of jobs. Exactness, concentration, fortitude, and sustained efforts will be demanded. White people have for generations had training in such jobs. They have been rehearsed in this type of discipline and they are therefore better prepared, both technically and emotionally, for this age of technology. You can no more expect one to walk in from a farm or out of a short-order kitchen prepared for such jobs than you can sneak daybreak past a healthy rooster. This is what the young Negro is asking for when he says that he no longer wants to be given the common, menial jobs but more of the jobs that call for higher skills and which provide bigger pay. This calls for a completely different concept of "job."

Professor Lucius F. Cervantes of Saint Louis University has another word on this topic. Regardless of how concerned we become about poverty, no matter how much we understand it, how many forces are brought to bear upon it, how successful the new rapprochement between Negro militants and the oak desk group may become, the young Negro must understand that today's jobs require an educational base that is inescapable. No one can get that for him.

Father Cervantes explains[4] that every emigrant group coming to America had to begin with the jobs on the bottom, whatever they were. But as opportunities opened they could filter through to better things. A new technology was not so widespread as to render them unemployable. Today, the Negro dropout may escape the color bar and then run head-on into the next hurdle, the education barrier. Quite apart from color discrimination, there is a shrinking margin of jobs for the untrained.

The population explosion is catching up with us at such a pace that the 73.6 million workers today will reach 87 million by 1970. This will squeeze even more untrained Negroes to the bottom.

The growth in automation is another ominous spectacle. Father Cervantes points to the Ford plant in Cleveland. Over 500 operations take place there with practically no human hands touching a half-mile link of 71 machines. Every hour 154 engine blocks are produced by 41 workers. Before automation it required 117. A bank in New York uses 90 specialists now to process the 600,000 checks that previously required 700 bookkeepers.

There are still areas of opportunity for high school graduates not yet threatened by computerization. The servicing and programming of the computers is one. The mountains of paper that the computers handle require clerks to prepare them and to handle them at the other end. There are still processes on both ends of the automated office.

The growth in the economy will cry out for persons to service our new gadgets and comfort devices. The expanding leisure for most workers means a growth in services related to recreation, fine arts, and travel.

The population boom and the auto traffic will call for the building trades and the construction trades in key population centers. Better incomes will be reflected quickly in personal services. All the jobs related to grooming, clothing, fashions, cosmetology, and so on will grow.

The nation's new emphasis on health and care for the aged and the poor will demand laboratory technicians, dental technicians, practical nurses, and medical aides.

The color problem will be with us, but, hopefully, in a rapidly diminishing form. As the civil rights leadership, the government, the churches, and public opinion continue to push the color barrier out of American economic life, the young Negro should prepare himself to find a place in the scheme of things. Every community effort that seeks to promote the idea of finishing high school is a very essential weapon in the war against poverty.

The poverty cycle is so well propelled by the thrust of discrimination, the initial force of the post-slavery identification of the Negro as a "hand," and the rhythm of weak education and low incomes, poor incentives, and rising technology that the task of overtaking its velocity is staggering. Yet it is so crucial to the total cause of Negro emancipation that nothing has higher priority. And, though the generalities abound, we may be sure that unless the combined forces of government, business, and Negro leadership can find an early answer the nation is flirting with danger. All one has to do is to drive through an urban ghetto and read the despair on the faces of hundreds of able-bodied men just sitting and looking, and he will see the danger. The avoidance of this danger and the prevention of a Watts make a valid but a second-best motive. Without the current threat of riots, sabotage, and social unrest, there should be among us a sufficient residuum of the wisdom from Athens, justice from Sinai, compassion from Galilee, courage from Lexington and Valley Forge, shame from Natchez and Chancellorsville, and awareness from Harlem and Watts to form a basis for prompt and effective action to break the poverty cycle.

6

Outliving the Stereotype

AS a working hypothesis, it is reasonable to set 1980 as the evaluation year, the time to make an assessment of how far the young Negro, who was a sit-inner in 1960, will goad his people up the road toward equality. What will the health statistics look like, desegregation in education, the crime rate, the housing patterns, the income comparisons, the test scores, the job patterns, and the increase in literacy? Using the year 1980 has the advantage of pinpointing the date when those who were sophomores in 1960 would be the parents of sophomores, one full generation. The millennium will not be here, of course, but the rate of change should be fantastic as compared with that of the period 1920 to 1940, or even from 1940 to 1960. This target date would show the adult of 1980 what he would need to accomplish during the last years of this century to guarantee that the twenty-first century will not find the Negro still wearing the badge of inferiority.

Negro Acceptance in Retrospect

Perhaps it is too much to speculate, but no significant change in the pace of Negro acceptance took place until 1960. It is sobering to observe how so much of history can pivot on a single incident. The Kennedys telephoned the wife of Martin Luther King to express concern over his arrest and incarceration during the 1960 presidential election, and this alone could easily have been sufficient to give President Kennedy that edge of the few thousand votes that gave him the plurality and the consolidation of the large, urban Negro vote in the big states. What would have happened if Richard Nixon had flown down to Atlanta and made a plea for King's release? What would have happened in 1876 had Tilden won the election instead of Hayes? What would have happened if the process of Reconstruction had not tapered off until after the Negro gains had been more completely solidified? Where would the Negro people be today, what would the face of America look like? Would our urban centers be such dungeons of despair funneling this endless procession to the abyss of futility? Suppose the Negroes had been permitted to keep and accelerate the pace for education and economic betterment that they had begun, without having to endure the torrents of vindictiveness that swept them backward soon after Hayes was elected President.

Lerone Bennett, Jr., senior editor of *Ebony Magazine,* that phenomenal journalistic success piloted by John H. Johnson, has given a brilliant description of the Hayes-Tilden showdown in his *Confrontation: Black and White.*[1] He calls it the beginning of the counterrevolution. There was widespread violence in the deep South as the whites were rapidly regrouping to check Negro progress in the 1870's. This "backlash" snapped the loudest in 1876 when in South Carolina, Florida, and Louisiana each party declared that it had won the election. These electoral votes meant the difference in the presidential election between the Republican, Rutherford B. Hayes from Ohio, and the Democrat, Samuel I. Tilden from New York. An Electoral Commission sustained the Republican claim, and Hayes won.

Meanwhile, the House of Representatives had to vote to validate the Commission's findings, and the South filibustered that vote until the last minute. What was the price that the Democrats from the South demanded to break the stalemate and let Hayes be inaugurated? It was the return of the South to white rule. This fateful decision was made on February 27, 1877, in the plush Washington hotel owned by a Negro family named Wormley.

On April 10, 1877, the federal soldiers turned Columbia over to white South Carolinians, and a few days later New Orleans was given over to white Louisianans. The curtain of denial and vengeance was drawn on a brief day of joy and hope for the black people, and daybreak is always slow for those who have lain anxiously awake through all the watches of the night.

For example, on March 1, 1875, a civil rights bill was passed. A Negro could travel and find lodging without discrimination under that bill. Wherever his money was good he could take his choice. He could sleep in the best staterooms on the steamboats, sit on the juries, and ride anywhere on the railroad trains that his ticket called for. He could sit anywhere in the theaters that he could afford. Between 1876 and 1894, fifteen Negroes sat in the North Carolina State Senate and fifty-two in the House. Had the franchise been restored to the whites without taking it from the Negroes, this picture surely would have changed, but not so dramatically as it did change. Negroes were voting and had developed political strength; but after the Hayes election they were whipped, mobbed, and beaten when they turned up at the voting places. The reversals in the fortunes of the black people were far from the result of the normal gravitation of human responses. Whites who argue today that integration should not be forced and that groups should fall naturally into their own homogeneity freely and without interference have short memories. They have forgotten how segregation was invented and forced!

The large numbers of Negroes in the South made the whole problem of the control of the life and movement of Negroes one of critical proportions. North Carolina, the most liberal and the most advanced of the southern states in terms of the treatment of Negroes, had in 1860 a population ratio, whites to Negroes, of two-to-one. This has remained steady ever since, for today the Negroes are still one-third of the North Carolina population. So, when a program of hate had to be made to work, the goal was to learn to hate every third person that one met or saw at a distance.

It was no ordinary task, therefore, to perfect the technique of keeping 300,000 black people down so completely and for such a long period that there would never be any question in the minds of the 600,000 whites that these people were born inferior. The correlation between the black face and inferior status was intended to be so complete that one would never know whether he was down because he was black, with a natural proclivity for things of low degree, or that he was deliberately put into an inferior status to show contempt for his racial origin.

Many a white man must have wondered why on earth his great-grandfather ever got involved in the slave business, but his great-grandfather never dreamed that the weight of morality and history would be on the side of the black people with such force that the white conscience could not rest until slavery was abolished. His great-grandfather never dreamed also that once they were free, these Negroes would be propelled by an intrinsic feeling of their own dignity to flee like a gazelle from everything reminiscent of a slave status. In the early days of slavery, 1699, a white man was rewarded for bringing slaves into the South. For each slave over 14 years old brought into North Carolina, fifty acres of land was given to the owner. Great-grandfather had something wonderful going for him except for one thing: he was unaware that he was dealing with human beings, creatures of God who would soon discover in their own simple way that over all men there was but one sky, one justice, one destiny.

The laws which the South began to pass after the fateful election of Rutherford B. Hayes did no more than codify their hatred. The actual date that a law is enacted is hardly indicative of the moral commitment of the people at a given political moment. The passing of a law may lag behind the congealing of sentiment for the law, on the one hand; and, on the other hand, the law may be passed at a politically opportune moment far ahead of the sentiment of the people who will have to live with that law. Today there is still some fear that the young Negro is a little naïve about what a law can accomplish. A bill passed by Congress represents a political victory at a given moment, often the result of a tug-of-war that eventuates in pulling one side across a razor-edged legislative line. Laws involving major changes in societal patterns are not the result, necessarily, of a consensus but hopefully an act of responsible men representing the people who may know full well that they are acting far in advance of the movement of social forces at the grass roots. These representatives often respond to power blocks that may be motivated by all kinds of considerations that lie outside the periphery of readiness in the hearts and minds of common folk. Thus, a legal proscription may not reflect the willingness of the people to follow or to comply.

William M. Kunstler, writing in *The Nation*, December 26,

1964, regarding his participation in a demonstration in the South, said this: "I no longer know where the movement ends and the law begins. In fact, for me now there is no significant dividing line. The movement has given my life heightened meaning and purpose. In return, I have put at its disposal all the energies I possess. I hope that the exchange is not too greatly in my favor." As the caldron of social change boils, no one knows exactly at what point it will harden into law because laws emerge at points of political advantage which are not always accurate reflections of a given plateau in social change.

There are times, however, when the laws so clearly reflect the feeling of the people that they are passed virtually by public acclamation. Thus, after the Hayes election, laws were passed in rapid succession to strip the Negroes of every gain that they had made and to assign them to a fixed position of political, social, and economic disadvantage. The first of these laws was passed to regulate elections. They gave wide powers to registrars and election judges. An appointed election judge could just about determine who would be permitted to vote and who would be denied. Obviously this was designed to deny Negroes the ballot. When this did not work, other forms of violence were persuasively used to frighten Negroes away from the polls. That was the mere beginning. In every aspect of life the Negro was compelled to roll back his gains.

Once the art of segregation and discrimination was learned, it was practiced with great skill. It was so pervasive that the best people were blind to its moral perversity and looked upon it as morally correct. They sought to find ways to be kind and gentle but always within the pattern of total segregation and discrimination. Albert Bushnell Hart, the famous Harvard educator at the turn of the century, commented in 1882 that he heard a man of some stature in the South say that they did not "want the Negroes to get educated, or to get rich; the more educated they are and the richer they are, the worse it is for us. . . . It is the big stick in their hands."[2] These attitudes were not merely matters of polite parlor conversation. They found their way into public policy and served as controlling forces in the day-by-day processes of life. And wherever the results of this thinking affected public policy, it had an immediate and devastating consequence in the lives of Negroes.

For example, there is in the composite stereotype of the southern Negro a picture of him as a dangerously unhealthy person. The inference is that he is too ignorant and careless to know what preserves good health. This has followed him all the way to the point of being denied insurance policies by major companies at regular rates. But, if one should go back and see how political impotency left a community helpless in protecting themselves against diseases, he could see how the Negro accumulated such terrifying health statistics. In Wilmington, North Carolina, in 1879, there were 341 deaths reported for Negroes. There were only 164 for whites. The Negroes were only one-third of the population. On the surface it would appear that the Negroes were a serious health menace. But because of their political weakness and their poverty they could do nothing about the fact that wells were dug only twenty or thirty feet from privies, and the soil in that community near the ocean was very permeable. In one square mile there were over 1300 shallow privies. The yearly water tax was $15 to $20, and the destitution of the Negroes prevented them from having city water made available. In 1880, the North Carolina Board of Health said that the water that the Negroes were drinking was dangerous from sewage contamination.

Prejudiced observers would never lay the above facts about wells and privies down beside the report of the mortality rate and make it clear that Negroes were being killed by water contamination. To the contrary, such figures are used to prove that Negroes are a weak, inferior race of people whose intermingling with others would cause a general deterioration of health standards. This would never be related to the fact that mean and callous politicians prevented these people from having clean water as they were herded together in a square mile, drinking filthy water from wells contaminated constantly by seepage from privies a few feet away.

The modern day "ultra-right winger," who calls the young Negro a communist stooge for marching the city streets protesting discrimination, needs to know about things like this, for he has been misled by tons of bad statistics on the Negro into believing that social change should take a long, slow, natural pace without "cramming the niggers down our throats." He needs to be reminded that the deprivations that the Negroes suffered did not come about by any *long, slow, natural* process. These disadvantages were thrust upon him by the *deliberate* actions of *conniving* people who wanted *to guarantee* his inferior status.

The decades 1900–1920 saw the Negroes on their knees, leaning heavily on religion as an asylum from brutal and relentless ostracism, lynching, and subjugation. The lights were out, the orators were dry in their throats, and the future was ominous. The reversals had come, and their sanguine hopes had turned to anemic despair. The philosophy of Booker T. Washington, his tacit acceptance of a society of separation and a program of prudence, with token gestures from a benign, guilt-ridden philanthropic class was an authentic commentary on the times.

The decades of 1920 to 1940 saw the hope that had died resurrected, the dawning of a renaissance movement, the glamor and pageantry of a Marcus Garvey, the growth of national protest organizations, a flirtation with socialism, the beginning of bold lawsuits, and the challenge of Franklin D. Roosevelt and the New Deal to take another breath and give America another chance.

Giving Color a New Content

We have seen this new vintage of the American Negro emerge in 1960; we have examined the responses that his activities called forth; we have looked at the young Negroes who are bogged down in futility, who are largely not college-bred and who represent the depths of deprivation; we turned then to look at the educational deficits that had to be overcome and the patterns of poverty that will have to be broken. Now we come to the stereotype that the young Negro will have to outlive.

To be quite blunt about it, the civil rights movement, the Supreme Court, the churches, the foundations, and the business community can make high resolves and set forth large, effective, and creative programs for change; but how much change can be expected of human nature? How indelible is the imprint of the Negro stereotype in the minds of the American majority? How can this stereotype be made to fade? How can the young Negro give a new content to color?

A young Negro college professor was at a student conference at the University of New Hampshire in the summer of 1951 when teachers who were on that campus in a summer program with pre-school children asked him to come over to the laboratory school so that the little white children could see a real Negro—live, kicking, and breathing. Many of their infant charges had never seen a Negro. The teachers were sincere in their simple request, and the Negro college professor complied with understanding. He went over to their laboratory classroom, had a monosyllabic talk with the children, and absorbed their gazes of astonishment as their mouths hung wide open and their eyes were brimming full with this new spectacle: a whole Negro.

When the professor left, the teachers made a record of their juvenile, innocent comments. One little girl said: "I like brown. My dress is brown." Another said: "Why can't the brown people and the white people get along?" "I have a brown and white cocker spaniel and I think brown and white go good together." Still another said: "I have on brown and white shoes and I think they are pretty." In these tender minds, far removed from the heavy traffic of the main American social arteries, there had been no identification of a Negro with anything but the neutral color *brown*. No content had been poured into the color *brown*. They had no reaction to a *brown* person because they had never seen how social customs and economic discrimination had succeeded in welding all the least desirable qualities of human life to brown persons. Most of those New England children will remain in small communities tucked securely away from the strong currents of prejudicial thinking.

Melting the Iceberg of Prejudice

But white youngsters growing up in other communities with large Negro populations, where the habits of discrimination and segregation are indelible, where the identification of the Negro with the worst in American life has been thoroughly accomplished, carry into their teens and on into their adulthood blind convictions that will not easily change. This is what the young Negro is up against as he seeks to change status. This iceberg of prejudice blocking his path at midstream will not melt easily. Many Negroes who have avoided contact with unemancipated whites have no idea of the depths of inertia that are grooved into the involuntary neurological patterns of response to the Negro's desire to innovate society. Many millions of whites react negatively to Negroes without taking any more thought than it would require to breathe.

A Negro minister happened to be seated with Billy Graham on a flight from Washington to Charlotte, North Carolina. On arrival in that gateway to the South, Dr. Graham invited the minister to come to his home on one of the peaks of the Appalachian ranges near Montreat. After some arranging, a suitable time to meet was agreed upon, and the two parted in the Charlotte airport as travelers delayed the ticket agents while they sneaked long stares at the handsome, impeccable Dr. Graham talking softly with this Negro wearing eyeglasses and a clean shirt.

The minister was then picked up by a North Carolina Negro educator who drove him to a Southern Baptist conference at Ridgecrest. As they sped along the clean, smooth black-top roads of North Carolina reminiscing over old times and anticipating their visit with Billy Graham the next morning, they felt a little gnawing hunger and pulled aside for a sandwich at a roadside eatery. This was in mountain-ribbed, rural North Carolina, thirty miles from even a small town. The Civil Rights Bill had been passed, and this small establishment was legally obliged to serve them. But the woman proprietor came out and announced to them in her mountain drawl that she would be mighty glad to bring a sandwich and a cup of coffee out to the car, but she wasn't ready to serve them inside yet. She said that she hadn't made up her mind what she was going to do about the Civil Rights Bill. This is a microscopic view of the entire problem. No doubt she was a Bible-reading, praying, dues-paying, "testifying" member of some fundamentalist church. She loved her Lord, but she had not made up her mind that she was going to change her image of colored people and accept them at her counter to eat a sandwich and drink coffee side by side with white farm laborers and truck drivers who would be stopping by her place.

If one saw that sweet-faced lady standing out in front of her place of business he could never imagine that so large a part of her psychological syndrome was this rigid resistance to a changed status of colored people. The young Negro has this rude awakening waiting for him, for the more zealous the Negroes are in changing conditions, the more they will hear housewives on these audience-response radio programs throughout the North and the South, giving their names and addresses and telling in subtle ways how much they hate Negroes. All one has to do is to watch carefully the semantic word games, the use of phrases like "states' rights," "law and order," "support your local police," and he will be amazed at what he hears.

This reaction may be labeled "backlash," but it is nothing but a revelation of what was already there, latent and dormant, which was aroused and strengthened when the Negroes began to make their bid for equal treatment. Ever since the Emancipation and throughout those days when the Negroes were making a fast start for full participation in American life, these have been the attitudes that they had to live with day in and day out. A well-educated Negro North Carolina senator in 1887 stood on the floor of that body and made this remark: "God speed the day when Carolina shall be free from . . . Negro haters. . . . I have never spoken in this Chamber unless aroused by flings at the Negro race. The sooner the whites of this state learn to respect the rights of my people, then will come the joyful day for us all."[3] Very deliberate efforts were made from the beginning to get the Negro used to humiliation.

During this heyday of Reconstruction power, a Negro in the First Congressional District of North Carolina was denied an opportunity to run on the Republican ticket and he became irate. There were in his district 13,000 Negro voters against 1,400 whites, and for twenty years the Negroes had waited for an opportunity to run for public office. His white friends told him that he was too "fresh."

As late as 1954, when a Negro preacher in a small eastern Carolina community decided to run for the County Board of Supervisors, his creditors insisted on the $8,000 that he owed them on a demand note. They loaned money on such notes in order to keep a noose around the necks of Negroes that could be drawn tight whenever they decided to step out of the role into which the whites had cast them. The Negro has had his place and he has not been able to step out of it with impunity.

The unfavorable image of the Negro which is projected today was not created by the normal flowing of social forces. It was a drydock fabrication. It was invented, constructed, and planned diabolically. A sample of the early formulation of the white position on the freed Negroes may be seen in the following comment printed in the *Winston Republican* on June 6, 1878: "It is a great mistake to suppose that the southern white man has any hostility to the Negro as a race. In his place, in a menial or service relation, he is liked and appreciated."[4] These were not casual words.

New Skills in Human Relations

The issue before us is this: What can the young Negro do in order to be successful in changing this image which has indoctrinated the white majority with an unfavorable and hostile attitude toward the Negro? Will Americans of goodwill understand how the stereotype was created and be just as deliberate, just as determined, and just as skillful not only in correcting the conditions which produced the stereotype but in softening the attitudes and trying to establish a new climate of receptivity to the aspiration of Negroes?

One aspect of modern living which is greatly in the Negro's favor is the rapid development of a scientifically oriented, technological society, following the rules of science, with a merciless assault on superstition and unscientific opinion. This scientific trend demands that every schoolboy come to adopt sooner or later a predisposition to look for cause and effect in everything. He will ask the right questions, if he is bright enough, and will insist on scientific answers even to a social phenomenon. A youngster who can conceive of a physical universe so loyally law abiding that physicists can, through mathematical projections, plot the path of a Mariner satellite and send it whirling millions of miles out into space, sending back coded pictures with an antenna only four feet in diameter and with less than three-and-a-half watts of power—anybody who can conceive of that will never understand why the color of a person's skin should be an index to his character, his personality, or his innate human worth.

A high school science student has to comprehend what it means to send a radio signal traveling at the speed of light that circles the earth in less than one-seventh of a second. If he can grasp that, he is far less likely to swallow rumors about people without testing them. If psychiatrists and biochemists can put their heads together and come up with hydroxytryptophane to change the chemistry of the brain, if they are able to isolate damines that aid normal brain functioning and then discover monoamine oxidase that works against proper brain functioning, and proceed from that point to find a way to attack mental disorders with psychic drugs, such

ingenuity in approaching human problems is bound to spill over
eventually into the area of race, raise the proper questions, and
find the proper answers that will aid the young Negro in diluting
the venom of racism that so effectively impedes his progress
toward equality.

Introspection by Religious Institutions

Not only will the rapid spread of scientific orientation aid in
demythologizing the race situation, but religious institutions are
taking fresh views of their positions. They are engaged in a
cleansing introspection and they are discovering that in countless
ways they had been merely shepherding the faithful into sheep-
minded conformity to the prevailing mores. This is happening on an
ecumenical front: Jews, Catholics, and Protestants talking together
in quiet, mountain hideaways, away from telephones, supermarkets,
subways, and the trappings of the modern world. Rabbis are
looking hard at Christian clergymen, demanding answers to old
issues that long have alienated two major religious communities.
Biblical scholarship is bringing into question certain liturgical and
ecclesiastical formulae that have been accepted for generations.
Determined efforts are being made to beat through the layers and
crusts of theological metaphors and shibboleths to discover the
true substratum of ethical monotheism.

Through close examination of archeological finds, comparing
variant original manuscripts, probing into the literature of those
cultures that were neighboring to the Jews and studying that whole
area where the God of Abraham, Isaac, and Jacob seems to have
bent low over his world and dealt uniquely with his people, the
scholars hope to learn more surely what the prophet Micah meant
when he said that goodness before God required men to do justly
and to love mercy; what the writer of Jonah meant when he insisted that a Jewish prophet, a messenger of God to a pure nation,
should go preach to a mongrelized people like the Ninevites; what
the writer of Ruth really meant when he told of a lowly, outcaste
Moabite girl being taken in marriage by pure-blooded Boas; what
Jesus of Galilee meant when he told a Syro-Phoenician harlot that
her respectable accusers and would-be executioners were as guilty
as she; what the Apostle Paul meant when he declared that the
greatest of all virtues was charity; and what John meant when he

said that a believer could not love God aright without loving persons aright first.

This inquiry into the nature of religious presuppositions will expose ideas and practices that have no place among people whose deity is a moral Being who cannot be teased by costly organs or placated by sonorous voices of well-groomed divines while the ethic of love is superseded by the authority of white supremacy.

This process cannot be hidden from public view. All literate people will sooner or later catch up with what the clerics are thinking and doing; and they will come to realize that the nearer men come to the real truths of God, the closer they will come to each other. And the longer they dillydally around their separate vines and fig trees and argue over the tweedle-dee and tweedle-dum of theology, the longer they will remain separated and the more room they will give for peddlers of hate and bigotry to circulate among them and confuse the issues.

So, as religious institutions seek to purify themselves, they will offer less and less comfort to those devotees who have ushered God on the side of racist thinking. As Erikson says in *Youth: Change and Challenge,* ". . . there is much in ancient wisdom which now can become knowledge as in the near future peoples of different tribal and national pasts join what must become the identification of one mankind, they can find an initial common language. . . ."[5] It is an open secret that the catalogue of do's and don'ts and other surface items of our culture that cloak themselves in religion and have gone unchallenged for generations passing for decency do not necessarily constitute an index to goodness.

In addition to what may be accomplished by the voluntary private agencies, government, and business, the young Negro can count on this shakedown in religion and this advance in scientific thought to shed new light on the whole racial dilemma and at least this will cause people to question some of the conclusions in their hearts and minds on the basis of which they have discriminated against Negroes.

Changes in Stereotype—Counterfeit and Genuine

There is little that the young Negro can do to change the stereotype artificially, for acts of ostentation, pseudoprosperity and pseudo-intellectualism are all transparent and only serve to make his cause counterfeit.

It is unfortunately true that in their anxiety to change their status, many Negroes, like other striving minorities, succumb to the temptation to engage in ostentatious conduct and conspicuous consumption. An occasional evening of role playing is not too tragic except that this often reflects a deeper malady, an adolescent view of what it will actually take to change the status and to destroy the stereotype.

The seriousness of the problem does not begin to show in all its height, breadth, and depth until we examine what must happen to the Negro family. The roots of the disintegration of the Negro family extend into the slave system, when the Negro family unit was not recognized and the members of the family were sold away from each other. And throughout the years since slavery the Negro woman has gained ego strength as a kind of *major domo* in the white household, supervising the kitchen and the parlor, ordering around the houseboys, dealing with vendors, rearing children, and setting up menus for dinner, making arrangements for weddings, and hospitality for guests. This subtle fact of the Negro woman being "somebody," while her sons, brothers, and nephews, along with her husband, were having their ego strength drained away by the white male in the fields, at the stables, on the docks, and in the warehouses, is definitive. She was "Gertrude," "Mary," "Ella," or "my Mildred." He was "hey boy," "this nigger" or simply "come here." Her status was guaranteed as long as she made herself indispensable to the "madam." But the Negro male was regarded as the real threat to racial separation and he had to be kept firmly in a posture of cringing fear.

Thus, the Negro male entered his new role of the modern father, with full responsibility, in a state of shock. Every day at 5:30 P.M. he must take on a personality exactly opposite to the one that he wears from 8:00 A.M. to 5:00 P.M., and many men fail to switch roles successfully. They bring into the management of private affairs that numbness and that immunity to challenge that they need for survival all day.

Therefore, what we find in the Moynihan Report, *The Negro Family,*[6] is a series of variations on the theme of the Negro adult male, his fall and his pending rise. In nearly a quarter of Negro homes he is missing, one out of four of his offspring is born without his name, fourteen out of every hundred of his children are on welfare, he is four times more likely to be unemployed than his white neighbor, and his female counterpart is having four children to the white woman's three.

His children, poorly supported and reared in an atmosphere of psychological insecurity, do commensurately less well in school. Their personal insecurities render them easily susceptible to immediate gratification and escapes that involve dropping out of school, early introduction to sex, dope, crime, and other forms of creeping decay. Such victims eventually become part of the subject, the Negro male, and the cycle starts up again.

If the stereotype is tied to this process it means that it will require far more than showing movies, holding retreats, and passing resolutions. Jobs will have to be made available by government programs where the economy is sagging, training and placement must be accelerated, and new housing must hastily replace those old monuments to failure and humiliation. The young Negro male has to pledge to his posterity that he will educate himself to his full capacity, honor his womanhood, protect his children, and rear a generation that will look back on the statistics of the sixties as if it were shaking itself from a bad dream. The white majority must understand the urgency of this, remove the nagging impediments, and applaud the rise of the Negro male.

Moreover, as we read and ponder the Moynihan Report, it is important to observe that the absent, delinquent Negro male, whose household is falling apart without him, is a social effect rather than a cause. He is a result, a product, a dividend, the "fallout" from the phenomena of joblessness and depersonalization. Whereas the statistics may imply that he is a positive, causative factor in the chain of delinquency, he is a cause only in the sense that it is a chain in which the social antecedents to his own life are passed on to his offspring in geometric progression. The program that the slave institution and the subsequent years of discrimination outlined for him produced exactly what they were calculated to produce, a general weakness in self-determination and resourcefulness.

Nevertheless, the young Negro now has the facts. He knows that there is a correlation between family cohesiveness and the capacity of the next generation to cope with the world. There is no comfort in knowing how it came about, and no solution accompanies the blame-placing process. Just as education must be pursued at whatever level of readiness one finds himself, so the task of saving the family must be pursued in the Negro communities as a self-generating force despite the social factors that vitiate wholesome family life.

There is yet an unresolved dichotomy in Negro thought which may prove to be a costly delay. On the one hand, there has developed such resentment of white authority, white standards, and white symbols of success that anyone who advocates a program of simple emulation of white mores is ridiculed. There are some young Negroes, and their white partners, who violate conventions in dress and public manners as a calculated social irritant. They call attention to themselves by being conspicuously at variance with local modes and tastes. This is conceived of as an unmistakable show of contempt for "phoney" middle-class standards. This contempt, however, pressed to its logical extremity, will run the risk of causing the young Negro to be insulated not only by his legacy of deprivation but by a wall of heightening estrangement, rendering it twice as difficult for initiative to come from the majority community. As lethargic as humans are about understanding each other and seeking value in the life of another, it is useless to expect progress to be made by requiring those in the privileged status to penetrate the thickness of this shield of contempt that everyone knows is embraced deliberately to accentuate the facts of anger and resentment. So, those who are selling the young Negro on the virtue of resigning from *all* middle-class American mores, and who call it courage to resist those who want to fuse Negroes into the culture of the majority, need to estimate what this will cost the drive for full and early inclusion in the deep channels of American life away from the swamps of poverty and the eddies of despair.

The young Negro militant sees nothing in this approach but an apologetic, slow assimilation and an anesthetic to more vigorous protests. He could not care less about white response to Negro patterns and, moreover, his approach calls for a much tighter, more radical, time sequence than 1960–1980. He talks of tonight, tomorrow, and now. To be sure, such militancy is a part of a total strategy, but whenever one turns to this strategy he still has eventually to start programing at some point. As A. Philip Randolph said at the November 18, 1965, planning conference for the 1966 White House Conference on Civil Rights, "There will always be a need for demonstrations to make the public aware of racial injustice, but we cannot stay in the streets forever. There comes a time when we must retreat to the conference room. . . ."

If the total strategy is one showdown after another in the streets, on the courthouse steps, in the governor's office, or in Congress, when and on what terms is new business ever begun? It may be that the only answer is an underground and a terror squad, but with the present stage of Negro involvement in those very processes that would represent the targets—business, government, and the military—the possibility of such violent militancy becoming a total strategy is nil. After all, the Solicitor General of the United States is a Negro, and the Attorney General of Massachusetts is another Negro, Edward Brooks.

Much of the talk of violence is not from confirmed rebels, but the expression of indignation on the part of those who feel that there is no really viable alternative. This frightening show of indignation is like the unsightly afterbirth that nauseates the curious onlookers after delivery, but which was a necessary protective covering during the months of embryonic defenselessness. The young Negro has to create a boldness that keeps his ego intact in confrontation with motherly appeals for restraint and threats of reprisal from bigots in the streets. The afterbirth is ugly, but without it the infant life would have aborted and what began as the promise of a new beginning would have been a still birth.

The economic and political dependency of Negro communities means that the real outcome of such total strategy of violence would be a polarization by white resistance, the detraction of talent and resources from those programs that have some hope of success, a federal posture of support for "law and order" rather than one of support for a new society, and a long, hopeless detour for those young Negroes who have little education and no skills. In fact, with the legislation now on the books and the defensive role into which the racists are now being forced, it would be a great loss if the young Negroes cancelled out their present position and switched signals in favor of greater insularity, a higher, explosive temperature in the entire racial forum, and the drawing of battle lines, rather than pressing for full implementation of the legal gains already made. It may be argued that violence is, sadly, the only language that the country will listen to, but this must not be conceded.

The young Negro should continue to strengthen his selfhood as a black man, learn his history, appreciate his roots, and hold his head high. But he must be too smart to trade his goal of complete and equal inclusion in American life for the cultural isolation of an angry black world. The natural impulse to be angry, the understandable but blinding cynicism, and the poor record of the white power structure are all an invitation to withdraw, to forget ameliorative schemes and to come out fighting.

But it is too late for that. The years of the 1960's have given us a preview of what can happen when the Negroes show their impatience, when they articulate political strength, and when they make known their resolve to be free. The Negro has just learned his way through the labyrinth of politics and economics, and he must pursue a constructive course relentlessly as a prime option.

Unfortunately, most of those who deplore the thoughts of violence approach the issue out of fear alone and with no thought of changing the conditions that lead to violence. They hope to get rid of the fever without killing the virus.

Many nervous whites and trembling suburban Negro "leaders" quake at the reports of militant young Negroes studying guerilla tactics and building up supplies of arms. They freeze with horror at the thoughts of a black underground, maids drowning babies, trusted servants turning killers, and masses of Negroes shooting bystanders, clerks, and storekeepers in black ghettos.

When such gruesome predictions are heard, the astonished "leaders" exclaim vehemently that violence is self-defeating. They hasten to ascend to high moral plateaus, taking their stand along with the monumental ethical systems of the ages, proclaiming that moral ends cannot be achieved by immoral means. To this argument the young militant steps back and shakes his head slowly in incredulity. He steps forward with this question to the disciples of nonviolence: But where were these shaky ones when the horses stampeded the students from Alabama State College, when Lemuel Penn and Medgar Evers were gunned down, and the Chaney-Goodman-Schwerner massacre was performed? Were they indignant with outrage?

There is a natural and understandable polarization to racial issues. It is just as natural for militant black boys to talk of a revolt as it is for George Lincoln Rockwell and his storm troopers to stand on American soil and salute the picture of Hitler. What we need is a determined effort at the eradication of racial injustice in every town, an effort that will create an atmosphere in which the Rockwell mentality cannot thrive and the threat of bloody black revolts will evaporate.

Negroes, in spite of their long-suffering and reputed docility, have no natural propensity for nonviolence. A sophisticated theory of nonviolence is the result of tireless spiritual discipline such as Gandhi's, and what makes us think that the Negro is more capable of such discipline than the Klansmen? It is rank paternalism that causes frightened whites and timid, middle-class Negroes to feel that black youth should think of every alternative before they conclude that stabbing and shooting and burning will be necessary to effect genuine change. All the nervous energy and whispered conversations of denunciation of violence should be converted into positive concern for racial justice; and the noise about violence would be converted into shouts of praise and thanksgiving for a new America that honors her promises.

The Priority of Full Participation

Implicit in the whole integration effort is still a hunger and a thirst on the part of Negroes to enjoy what America offers, to be accepted, to be included. The quest for inclusion cannot possibly be a part-time love affair with American life. It will have to include jobs, housing, and equal educational and political opportunity; it will have to include further a loss of that identity acquired across the tracks and uptown in the ghetto and a new identity as a full American. As the old stereotype of the Negro dies, a new image will be born; and this will inevitably be an emulation of the best and the most enduring values in the dominant society.

It should be clear also that the America into which the Negro will integrate will not be the one that exists now. The process of change cannot be the mere pasting of middle-class merit badges on polite Negroes. It will be a society much less impressed with an aristocracy of blood or money than one of brains and character; there will be far more escalators leading deserving people out of poverty, and the upper levels of society will have many more who earned a niche there than those who happened to look up and find themselves born there; there will be Negro children carried to the symphony, not to see all white performers play all white music, but Negro performers, too, and some of the themes will come from Yoruba chants and Hausa cattlemen's songs; many of the museums and galleries will have Negro staff, and the suburban high school will have a Negro coach and a Negro biology teacher. Thus, the target for 1980 is an acceleration of present procedures by a considerable degree, not a longer stage of preparation and a delay of another twenty years. We are talking about a process that has already begun and whose culmination should be in sight by 1980. The question is, How much time will be lost in the deferment of this approach? In order for whites to give their hearts to the integration effort they will have to stop "thinking white" and start "thinking integrated." The Negro will have to undergo the same psychological metamorphosis.

The cause must not be lost on a gamble that a black chauvinism that detracts from the total effort toward inclusion and equality will suffice. Such energies should be turned toward the promising new political front.

The *New York Times*,[7] in reporting a luncheon at the Waldorf-Astoria Hotel, which celebrated the twentieth birthday of *Ebony,* quoted its founder and publisher, John H. Johnson, as follows:

" 'Today, achievement is measured in terms of whatever a man sets out to do,' [John H. Johnson] said.

"Mr. Johnson predicted that in the next twenty years Negro income, now $27 billion a year, would reach $75 billion.

" 'By 1985 we will probably have Negro mayors in two or three of our ten largest cities,' he added, 'Negro congressmen from the South, and perhaps even a Negro Vice-President.' "

By 1980, in retrospect, it will be much clearer than it is today that the 1965 Voting Rights Bill and the reapportionment of states to guarantee only one vote for each citizen were the most decisive developments induced by the young Negro in his quest for equality. In the long run, these will accomplish the spade work that nothing else could touch. Georgia has two Negro senators and four in the Georgia lower chamber. This is the beginning of that neo-emancipation, picking up what the election of 1876 abruptly ended. When Negroes do become visibly and undeniably a part of the real political life of the South, they will cause changes in the state capitols and in the county courthouses that will make a big difference. When they become aldermen and county supervisors all over the South, and represent Memphis, Jackson, Birmingham, New Orleans, Atlanta, Baltimore, and Houston in the Congress, then the color factor will become less and less determinative.

As the transition from static social accommodation to racism to vibrant social adjustment to equality proceeds, the rate of change will be uneven. There will be Negroes appointed to positions as agents of power who will discover that those who assigned them to such big jobs did not really want change but a peaceful stalemate. While such black power agents maneuver to convert their bosses and hold the confidence of their black compatriots, there will be ankle-breaking footwork and actual career suicide. It will not always work, and many who thought that they had the skill to walk this tightrope will end up as casualties. But this is a necessary component in the total machinery of change in racial patterns. This will have to go on until there is enough evidence that Negroes can accept positions of power without being well-to-do-Toms.

As the transition proceeds, many who enjoyed high acclaim as civil rights leaders will find it difficult to convert themselves into "mainstream" administrators. When the news broke that James Farmer was surrendering as the CORE executive to head a literacy training program, many high brows were arched in disbelief. But Farmer is merely symbolizing the nature of the change. It will involve an increased emphasis upon participation along with the continued emphasis upon protest. It would be extremely unfortunate and misleading if Farmer's action were taken as a capitulation or a "sell-out." He has a right to elect his own vocational priorities. But it would be a great mistake to confuse his move with a definitive understanding of the Negro mood. Literacy training and skills development are urgent needs. But mature Negroes know that these are derivative needs, and the more basic need is to rid the country of that pattern of racist thinking and practice which produced such a delinquency in literacy and such a dearth of skills training.

Inclusion and participation will indeed require literacy training, but there must be the cultivation of a spirit of openness toward Negroes at the same time, for the experience of Negroes is that highly trained Negroes who could read and write in several languages could not crack the color line. Dr. William T. Carter, recently the Peace Corps representative in Senegal and the holder of A.B., M.A., and Ph.D. degrees from the University of Michigan, reads, writes, and speaks Italian, French, German, and Spanish. And yet he was inducted into the army in 1940 as a private and held at that grade until General Eisenhower heard about him and ordered him to be commissioned in the field.

The young Negro needs now to acquire a tough sense of priority and a firm grasp of the factors that went into the creation of the Negro stereotype. He must keep his eye on all those movements and seek to pull out the threads from which the stereotype was woven. But he needs also to monitor the attitudes that yet prevail and to be sophisticated enough about what it will take to change these. He cannot go around chanting the chauvinist theme on "thinking black" and talking about integration at the same time. These two policies are mutually exclusive, and one cannot embrace black exclusivism on the one side and at the same time talk about finding his way into a full-fledged participant role in American life.

Integration will indeed cost the Negro this lingering ethnocentricity. Separation from ethnocentricity means the abandonment of a campaign to accentuate racial differences. This does not mean an abandonment of one's identification, occupying a no man's land as a racial nonentity, a crusade to intermarry and achieve a coffee-with-cream complexion compromise that gets rid of the black problem by getting rid of black. God forbid! Intermarriage is not a racial issue. It is a private, family affair. It has to do with falling in love, making pledges, shutting out the nosey world, and blending two private lives. It does not involve 20,000,000 people seeking freedom. The larger issue is how much of the racial stereotype is tied to racial consciousness, a feeling of being part of a community of people, and how much of it is the crust of incompetence baked on the race under the thermal waves of denial and subjugation. The issue is how much of the image of the Negro must be dissolved and lost without the concomitant loss of selfhood, of "soul," of continuity with one's own genetic stream, even though it may flow through the torrents of indignation, the lowlands of suffering, or to an open sea of a forgotten past.

It is a tragic fact that America has wrung from the hearts of too many Negroes every ounce of pride that racial impulses caused to flow. Like strangers and aliens they walk between the black and white world afraid to turn to the right or the left. A Negro should be able to close his eyes, clap his hands, pat his feet, and smile with deep content in a Sunday morning Baptist service when the choir takes an old Wesley hymn and changes its cadence into a rhythmic beat, where a moaning, tired sister is free to scream a "Thank you, Jesus!" and where the house is filled with the Spirit, without apologizing to a single, living soul. He should feel as relaxed about this as an orthodox Jew feels about buying kosher meat, a Quaker about his silent worship, a Catholic about his confessions, or a Moslem about his fasts.

There is room enough in America for everyone to be as particularistic as he wishes about his dress, his food, his music, his worship, his speech inflection, his jokes, his games, and how he spends his Saturdays. But this is quite different from assigning to one group a status that is immutable and that implies basic and changeless inferiority. It is different from a label assigned that tags one as intrinsically inferior because of racial origin.

Outliving the stereotype means rubbing off the stamp of shame. It does not mean dilution of one's heritage, changing his music, or scraping himself white. It means stepping out of the mire of bad statistics in those matters that affect any and all Americans, mortality rates, crime rates, financial competence, educational attainment, and political participation. It has nothing to do with whether one likes Wagner or Count Basie, whether he does the polka or the frug, whether he eats greens and yams or snails and frog legs.

When the young Negro is mature enough to embrace his Negritude without permitting it to insulate him from America, when he can sift out of American culture what he wants and leave the rest without rancor, when he can fight racism without losing the battle by stumbling on his own dangling hatreds, when he can bid high for inclusion without sacrificing his identity, demand a decent living without embracing the goddess of money, fight for housing without worshiping at the shrine of suburbia, walk in and out of America's institutions with a loyal patriotism but without condoning America's sins or blinding himself to her hypocrisies, not only is he effecting integration but America should marvel that after seven generations this measure of restraint and discipline is possible, signifying a strength the country needs.

Five Stages from Slavery to Freedom

The historical perspective that sets today's challenge to the young Negro in proper focus may be seen in five stages, tracing the path of the Negroes from the matrix of slavery to the threshold of freedom.

Stage one—Disintegration. During the first twenty-five years after the Emancipation Proclamation, society in the South may be described as disintegrated. During slavery it was integrated. The Negroes were part of the *integer*—the whole. They were involved in every aspect of the lives of the whites, but with a slave status. They were not separated physically. They were there, milking the cows, chopping the wood, drawing water from the well, nursing the babies, making the beds, cooking the food, and praying in the white man's church. After the Emancipation, with no money, no names, no culture that they could remember and with no place to go, the newly freed Negro roamed around in his ignorance and poverty until he found himself back on the farm in a modified form of slavery. The white South was in economic chaos, and the blindness of bitterness left it groping toward an ominous future.

Stage two—Alienation. When the Negroes decided to make a bid for real economic and social emancipation, they incurred the wrath of the whites. Then the lynchings began, the mob violence, and the vicious attacks on Negroes as a race. Negroes migrated en masse to Kansas and Indiana and other points in the North and West to escape the rage of the angry whites. They gathered at the railroad depots by the hundreds, with their meager belongings packed in bags and barrels of all shapes and sizes, trying to escape the vindictiveness of the whites after the South was given back to them.

Stage three—Imitation. This stage overlapped others, but it gained momentum around 1890. Negroes were establishing a replica of the white world when they were compelled to create their own society. Completely and unquestionably ousted from the white world, they went about building an entire society alongside that of their white neighbors. It was a copy of the white world in every detail—fraternities, cotillions, literary societies, and stores that sold "plain and fancy" groceries. They even learned how to elect delegates to send to conventions in England with expenses paid! Their colleges and universities were copies of the liberal arts white institutions. What else had they seen? And, in this effort, a strange providence was guiding them. What could four million people do better than to begin to prepare early, even in the unfortunate incubator of a segregated society, for an eventual return to the mainstream of American life, with equality. From their white neighbors they learned parliamentary procedure, how to stage musical and literary teas, and they carried this package of culture lock, stock, and barrel over to the other side of the railroad tracks and unwrapped it in their Negro society.

Stage three was the stage of imitation, rehearsing for eventual reintegration.

Stage four—Litigation. In 1883 the Civil Rights Bill of 1875 was repealed. But the Negroes did not give up. In 1896 a Louisiana mulatto named Plessy went to court to sue for his right to public facilities without discrimination. He lost the case on purely sociological speculation, on the same grounds that the white reactionaries said that the Negroes won the case in 1954. There was no issue at law underlying the decision, but the Supreme Court spoke in the language of the sociologists, holding that Negroes could enter white society only at the behest of the whites. But the Negroes were restless for the next thirty years and then they began the legal onslaught in the late 1930's and early 1940's against all public facilities that were segregated. After 39 successive victories, led by Charles Houston, Thurgood Marshall, James Nabrit, Oliver Hill, Spottswood Robinson, and an invincible armada of bright Negro lawyers trained largely at Howard University under the inspiration of Mordecai Johnson, there is now no legal basis for racial segregation in any aspect of American life where the general public has an interest.

Stage five—Reintegration. The Negroes have gone full cycle. They were locked out of the white world; they went off and constructed their own society; they came back and attacked the legal basis for their ostracism; and now they are on their way back in—but this time as first-class participants without conditions.

Here is the threshold on which the young Negro stands today. In order to accomplish this last stage, and with everything going for him, he must be prepared to resist the stubborn psychological barriers in the minds of the whites. This will be accomplished by showing the same courage in the areas of education, economics, and politics as was shown marching a thousandfold to the courthouse singing freedom songs. The latter has already been done, and with great effectiveness. Another type of achievement is called for now with another type of program.

The young men of Pentecost Island in the New Hebrides are introduced into adulthood with a ceremony that requires them to jump from a bamboo tower 40 to 90 feet in the air. They jump headfirst toward the earth with a long vine tied to their ankles at the one end and to the top of the tower at the other. This carefully measured vine breaks their fall a few inches from suicide. They fall through a frail thatch barrier on the way down to break the speed of their descent. This jump is designed to test their courage, their confidence in their fellow tribesmen who assist in building the tower and in preparing the long vine that saves their lives, and their skill in sprawling safely on the ground without breaking limbs. This is the kind of agility that it takes to live successfully on Pentecost Island in the New Hebrides. This is an adequate test to prove those who say that they are ready to move on their own as male, adult citizens on that Island. The style of life on Pentecost Island can be managed well by those who pass this test. But America has other tests for another style of life.

The young Negro will have to remain committed to integration and not make a psychological nest inside the Negro world to which he may revert when the going gets rough. He will have to commit himself to competitive participation in every American process and abandon the advantages that accrued to him as he excelled over his weaker Negro competitors within a segregated framework. He must wade into the world of white politics waist high, endure the insults, risk the loss of security, unravel the complicated issues, live with inconclusive answers to problems that defy immediate and obvious simplification and stay in there plugging until he can find his place in the halls of decision and become an integral part of the policy-making bodies of America. He must enroll his children in excellent schools shoulder to shoulder with their white neighbors and require them to exercise the diligence to keep the pace. He must have the courage to buy a house outside the ghetto and permit his white neighbors to discover that among all the things to be learned about a Negro family, the fact of their color is the least significant. He must educate and promote his women and call an early halt to the practice of liberal organizations that devise their ameliorative schemes and plan their programs with liberal white women and educated Negro men. He must compete for federal jobs where there is already more of a guarantee of the movement of competent people to the top so that hundreds of middle-class whites may have personal experience on the whole question of working under a Negro supervisor and alongside Negro colleagues.

In other words, under the most favorable conditions the young Negro will find it a real task to overcome his educational deficit, change the poverty pattern, and outlive the American stereotype of the Negro. If he plays for keeps, he will succeed; and in 1980 he will look back and see that he has come a very, very long way. He will look his grandson in the face and tell him with confidence and assurance that there is no longer a penalty for being born of darkened hue. He will recount the victorious pilgrimage through 250 years of human bondage, and 100 more years of repression and defeat, to the high plateau of equality and real freedom. He will explain how persistently the black population pressed for equality and inclusion, how relentlessly they compelled the nation to reappraise her slogans and customs and reexamine her institutions and practices until at last the promises of the Bill of Rights and the guarantees of the Constitution were honored for all her people.

It is important for America that the young Negro should succeed. His crusade has called us to renovate all our racial practices and to re-examine the value hierarchy that we have taken for granted in the United States. As he proceeds, this scrutiny of our common life will be intensified, and his cause will become a kind of barium, flowing through the viscerals of our society, revealing to us our ruptures, fissures, and cancerous growths, and the other impediments that must yield to the surgery of the truly democratic ideal.

General Sarnoff of RCA promises that within a little while each one of us will be able to carry a vestpocket transmitter and receiver that will connect to a switchboard linked to communications satellites orbiting in space. The satellites will decode and transmit billions of arrangements of pulses, everyone having his own signal. There is space enough for these channels and there is the technological know-how today to put everyone of us in touch with anyone else in the world in a matter of seconds. If this is the way the world is going to be, it will be one preposterous incongruity to have in this kind of world persons living side by side on that blessed and richly endowed patch of earth called America who cannot find a way to lay aside old habits of hurting each other and to guarantee an equal opportunity for everyone. Let us rejoice over the growing evidence that a free society, with equality for everyone under the law, is possible and imminent, and that it is more and more acknowledged to be inexorably our only hope.

Notes by Chapters

Chapter 1

1. Harry L. Golden, *Mr. Kennedy and the Negroes* (Greenwich, Conn.: Fawcett Publications, Inc., 1964).
2. Kenneth B. Clark, *Dark Ghetto* (New York: Harper & Row, Publishers, Inc., 1965), p. 177.
3. L. D. Reddix, *Crusader Without Violence* (New York: Harper & Brothers, 1959), p. 205.
4. In James Baldwin, *Nobody Knows My Name* (New York: Dial Press, Inc., 1961), p. 26.

Chapter 2

1. Robert W. Spike, *The Freedom Revolution and the Churches* (New York: Association Press, 1964), p. 104.

Chapter 3

1. Simeon Booker, *Black Man's America* (Englewood Cliffs, N.J.: Prentice-Hall, Inc., 1964), p. 73.
2. From a pamphlet entitled *Mission for a World of Cities,* a speech delivered by Harvey Cox on May 20, 1965, in San Francisco at the American Baptist Convention.
3. Baldwin, *op. cit.,* p. 60.
4. *Social Action,* Nov., 1964, p. 27.

5. Saul Bernstein, *Youth on the Streets* (New York: Association Press, 1964), p. 62.
6. Martin Luther King, *Stride Toward Freedom* (New York: Harper & Brothers, 1958), p. 107.
7. Hubert H. Humphrey, *War on Poverty* (New York: McGraw-Hill Book Co., Inc., 1964), pp. 84 ff.
8. Michael Harrington, *The Other America: Poverty in the United States* (New York: The Macmillan Company, 1962), p. 20.
9. *Information Service,* National Council of Churches, No. 7, XLIV, 3.
10. Saul Bernstein, *op. cit.*
11. Simeon Booker, *op. cit.,* p. 192.

Chapter 4

1. Whitney Young, *To Be Equal* (New York: McGraw-Hill Book Co., Inc., 1964), p. 102.
2. Frenise A. Logan, *The Negro in North Carolina, 1876–1894* (Chapel Hill, N.C.: The University of North Carolina Press, 1964).
3. *Ibid.,* p. 139.
4. Whitney Young, *op. cit.,* p. 133.
5. Kenneth B. Clark, *Dark Ghetto* (New York: Harper & Row, Publishers, Inc., 1965), pp. 117–118.
6. Simeon Booker, *op. cit.,* p. 141.
7. Clark, *Dark Ghetto* (New York: Harper & Row, Publishers, Inc., 1965), p. 131.
8. *Ibid.,* p. 128.
9. Dr. Otto Klineberg, *Negro Intelligence and Selective Migration* (New York: Columbia University Press, 1935).

Chapter 5

1. See Frenise A. Logan, *op. cit.,* p. 93.
2. Published by the Southern Regional Council, Oct. 18, 1965.
3. Logan, *op. cit.,* p. 84.
4. Lucius F. Cervantes, *A Better Education . . . A Better Job* (New York: American Press, 1965).

Chapter 6

1. (Lincoln, Neb.: Johnsen Publishing Co., 1965), pp. 85 ff.
2. Logan, *op. cit.,* p. 140.
3. *Ibid.,* p. 154.
4. *Ibid.,* p. 1.
5. Erik Erikson, *Youth: Change and Challenge* (New York: Basic Books, Inc., 1963), pp. 22–23.
6. Department of Labor, March, 1965.
7. *New York Times,* November 30, 1965.

DAT